A-LEVEL YEAR 2

STUDENT GUIDE

OCR

Economics

Microeconomics 2

Sam Dobin

PHILIP ALLAN FOR
HODDER
EDUCATION
AN HACHETTE UK COMPANY

Philip Allan, an imprint of Hodder Education, an Hachette UK company, Blenheim Court, George Street, Banbury, Oxfordshire OX16 5BH

Orders
Bookpoint Ltd, 130 Park Drive, Milton Park, Abingdon, Oxfordshire OX14 4SB

tel: 01235 827827

fax: 01235 400401

e-mail: education@bookpoint.co.uk

Lines are open 9.00 a.m.–5.00 p.m., Monday to Saturday, with a 24-hour message answering service. You can also order through the Hodder Education website: www.hoddereducation.co.uk

© Sam Dobin 2016

ISBN 978-1-4718-5688-4

First printed 2016

Impression number 5 4 3 2 1

Year 2020 2019 2018 2017 2016

This Guide has been written specifically to support students preparing for the OCR A-level Economics examinations. The content has been neither approved nor endorsed by OCR and remains the sole responsibility of the authors.

Typeset by Integra Software Services Pvt. Ltd., Pondicherry, India

Cover photograph: Iakov Kalinin/Fotolia

Printed in Italy

Hachette UK's policy is to use papers that are natural, renewable and recyclable products and made from wood grown in sustainable forests. The logging and manufacturing processes are expected to conform to the environmental regulations of the country of origin.

Contents

Content Guidance

Questions & Answers

■ Getting the most from this book

Exam tips

Advice on key points in the text to help you learn and recall content, avoid pitfalls, and polish your exam technique in order to boost your grade.

Knowledge check

Rapid-fire questions throughout the Content Guidance section to check your understanding.

Knowledge check answers

1 Turn to the back of the book for the Knowledge check answers.

Summaries

■ Each core topic is rounded off by a bullet-list summary for quick-check reference of what you need to know.

Exam-style questions

Commentary on the questions

Tips on what you need to do to gain full marks, indicated by the icon **e**

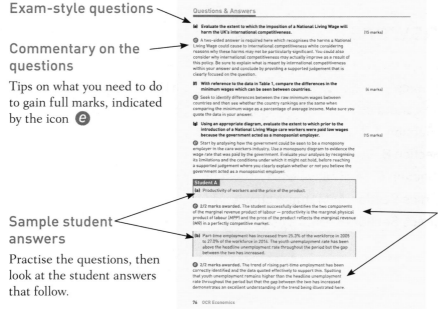

Commentary on sample student answers

Find out how many marks each answer would be awarded in the exam and then read the comments (preceded by the icon **e**) following each student answer. Annotations that link back to points made in the student answers show exactly how and where marks are gained or lost.

Sample student answers

Practise the questions, then look at the student answers that follow.

■ About this book

This guide is designed to prepare you for the A-level OCR Microeconomics exam and the A-level OCR Themes in Economics exam. It includes sample questions and answers to prepare you for both papers. In addition to the content covered here, you will also need to be familiar with the content in *Student Guide 1* to sit the A-level Microeconomics exam and the content in *Student Guides 1, 2* and *4* in order to sit the A-level Themes in Economics exam.

The guide is split into two sections:

Content Guidance

This section explains the core microeconomics concepts required to excel in this course. This can be split into four broad topic areas:

■ Scarcity and choice
■ Competition and market power
■ The labour market
■ Market failure and government intervention

You should make sure you have fully mastered all of the content in this guide before progressing onto the practice questions. Use the Knowledge checks as you progress through the guide to test your understanding and take on board the comments to avoid falling into the traps which most commonly result in students losing marks. At the end of each topic area there is a bullet pointed summary of the content covered – if you are unable to offer a detailed explanation of any part of this you should read the section again to clear up any misunderstanding.

Questions & Answers

This section begins by setting out the format of the exam papers, giving you advice on how long to spend on each question and offering important tips on how to maximise your marks on the different elements of the paper. It also explains the levels system used to mark essays.

This is followed by a series of sample questions. After all of these questions there are some example answers from students. You should practise all of these questions yourself and compare your answers to these while reading the detailed comments to improve your understanding of what is required to achieve full marks.

Content Guidance

■ Scarcity and choice

The concept of the margin

The concept of the margin is crucial in understanding how economists model decision making. The marginal principle suggests that individuals make decisions by considering the impact of small changes from the existing situation, essentially making tiny adjustments to their behaviour in order to achieve the best possible outcome. The concept of opportunity cost is, of course, based upon this principle, where an individual makes a choice in favour of something that delivers them greater benefit than the next best option. The margin can therefore be used to model decision making on both an individual and a societal level:

- Individuals weigh up the marginal benefit against the marginal cost of an action when deciding whether to proceed with that action. Individuals will proceed only when the marginal benefit exceeds the marginal cost, as it is in this instance that they will be better off from taking the action. When the marginal cost exceeds the marginal benefit they would be better off not proceeding, meaning individual behaviour remains unchanged when the marginal benefit equals the marginal cost, as there is no incentive to change the decision in this instance.

- Social optimum is arrived at using the same logic, occurring where marginal social benefit is equal to marginal social cost. We know from our study of market failure that this social optimum is sometimes not reached — for example, in the case of healthcare, the marginal social benefit would exceed the marginal social cost if provision of this service were left to the free market.

Knowledge check 1

Why is the social optimum of marginal social benefit equals marginal social cost unlikely to be reached if healthcare provision were left to the free market?

Marginal utility theory

Economists refer to the satisfaction individuals derive from consuming a particular good or service as utility. The concept of utility can be used to explain the slope of the demand curve. Because individuals make decisions on the margin, we need to look at the marginal utility deriving from the consumption of a good or service — the additional utility gained from consuming an extra unit of a good or service. This gives rise to the **law of diminishing marginal utility**, which proposes that as consumption of a good increases, the benefit you derive from consuming each additional unit decreases.

Consider the example of purchasing a car. Individuals derive significant utility from the first car they own — without this first car, they would find it much more difficult to go about their daily lives. Wealthy individuals might decide to purchase a second car. While they enjoy some utility from this — for example, it enables them to drive a small car for city trips and a larger car for family holidays — the additional utility this second car brings is clearly smaller than that of the first car. By the time the individual purchases a third car the additional utility has diminished further — utility is enjoyed only on the one occasion a year when both of the other cars are being

Law of diminishing marginal utility The more units of a good that are consumed, the lower the utility from consuming those additional units.

repaired. This simple principle of diminishing utility can be applied to the consumption of all goods and services.

This therefore explains why the demand curve is downward sloping — the price an individual is willing to pay for a good or service decreases the more of it they consume as consumption becomes increasingly less valuable to them because of the diminished utility they enjoy from additional units of consumption. As illustrated in Figure 1, if a monetary value could be placed on utility, the price an individual would be willing to pay to consume Q^* units of the good would be equal to the marginal utility (MU^*) the individual derives from consuming the final unit of output. They would only be willing to consume more than Q^* at a lower price because the marginal utility of consuming more units would be lower than MU^*.

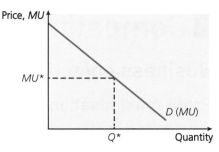

Figure 1 Demand and marginal utility

Rationality

Using the concept of the margin to model the behaviour of economic agents is based on the assumption that rationality holds — economic agents always do what they expect brings the best possible results. However, behavioural economists argue that this is an unrealistic assumption, citing many examples of situations when consumers make decisions that are not in their best interests and firms make decisions that cannot be seen as profit maximising. This is because economic factors are not the sole influence on decision making — individuals often act on impulse in response to their feelings. The impact of emotion on decision making is ignored by marginal analysis, yet is clearly important in understanding how individuals behave.

A simple example of this can be seen in how individuals behave while doing their weekly supermarket shop. Assume utility can be measured in monetary terms and an individual derives £2 utility from consuming one bag of oranges and £2.80 utility from consuming the second bag of oranges. The supermarket is selling bags of oranges on a promotional deal of 'Buy one get one half price', with the full price being £1.80. If the individual were behaving rationally they would purchase just one bag of oranges — the decision to purchase a second bag at a price of 90p is not rational because they derive only 80p utility from the consumption of that bag (£2.80 – £2). However, many individuals faced with such a choice will purchase the second bag as they are drawn towards the special offer. Such emotional decision making goes against the concept of the margin.

Knowledge check 2

Is giving money to charity evidence of individuals behaving rationally?

Summary

After studying the topic of *Scarcity and choice* you should be able to:
- Explain what is meant by the concept of the margin and understand how marginal values can be calculated from a set of data.
- Understand how the marginal concept can be applied to the decision making of economic agents.
- Evaluate the extent to which individuals behave rationally and therefore whether the concept of the margin is useful to economists in explaining the decision making of economic agents.

■ Competition and market power

Business objectives

Profit maximisation

One of the most fundamental assumptions economists make in constructing the theory of the firm is that firms aim to maximise profits. Profit can be calculated as follows:

Profit = Total Revenue − Total Cost

A firm is said to be making a normal profit when:

Average Revenue = Average Cost or Total Revenue = Total Cost

At first glance this may seem confusing — how can a firm be making a profit when its revenues are only equal to its costs? This can best be explained by an example. Suppose an accountant quits her £50,000-a-year job to set up a bakery. The total revenue of her bakery is £95,000 and the total cost (costs of premises, employees, ingredients, electricity etc.) is £45,000. To say the individual enjoys a £50,000 profit from running the bakery would, however, be incorrect, as it is ignoring the individual's opportunity cost. In choosing to run the bakery the individual is sacrificing the £50,000 she could have earned as an accountant. Economists include this opportunity cost — essentially the cost of enterprise — in total cost, meaning in this instance the bakery is earning a normal profit. Any profits made by a firm above this level are known as abnormal or supernormal profits.

The profit-maximising level of output occurs when marginal revenue (MR) equals marginal cost (MC). This can be proven by explaining why all alternative levels of output would not be profit maximising. If marginal revenue exceeded marginal cost, the change in total revenue as a result of increasing output by one unit would exceed the change in total cost as a result of increasing output by one unit, meaning more profit could be made by increasing output. Similarly, when marginal cost exceeds marginal revenue, firms are making a loss on the production of the last unit of output, meaning profit could increase by reducing output. The profit-maximising level of output therefore occurs when $MC = MR$.

Alternative maximisation objectives

In some circumstances firms may choose to maximise something other than profits. Examples of such alternative maximising objectives are:

- *Revenue maximisation* — many managers are paid salaries that are related to total revenue rather than profits. This therefore incentivises managers to aim to maximise revenue rather than profit. Production will take place where $MR = 0$. Clearly a revenue-maximising firm will produce a higher level of output than a profit-maximising firm, as it will continue to produce output even when $MC > MR$ providing total revenue is still increasing (i.e. $MR > 0$).
- *Sales maximisation* — when managers are paid salaries related to the volume of sales they may be incentivised to sales maximise. This may lead to even greater

> **Exam tip**
>
> The profit-maximising condition is crucial in constructing all of the theory of the firm diagrams — memorise it and make sure you fully understand why profits are maximised at the level of output where $MC = MR$.

output than in the revenue-maximising case, as firms will continue to increase output even if total revenue is falling as total sales will be increasing. They will continue to do this until the point where Total Revenue = Total Cost, beyond which the firm would have to close down.

■ *Growth maximisation* — a manager's reputation will be enhanced if they oversee significant growth of the firm. To achieve this they are likely to follow a similar strategy to that outlined above, where they will continue to produce output until they are making a normal profit. band loyalty , Increase market share

■ *Utility maximisation* — there is evidence that some managers will set out to maximise satisfaction. Satisfaction can be derived in a number of ways. For example, they may be prepared to forgo high levels of profits or sales in order to have a large office and expensive company car. In some instances, managers might even be seeking to maximise the utility of their consumers when making business decisions.

The principal–agent problem

As indicated above, it is when managers are not incentivised by profit that they will pursue alternative objectives. This is most likely to occur in large firms, particularly public limited companies, which are owned by a large number of shareholders. In these firms there is a separation between ownership and control. The owners (the shareholders) are motivated by profit, but they are not the people with the control over the day-to-day running of the business (the managers). This creates what is known as a principal–agent problem — the principal (shareholders) delegates decision making to the agent (managers), but the agent has different motivations from the principal and therefore may take decisions that are not in the principal's best interests. Clearly, this problem occurs only when such a separation between ownership and control exists — in small firms, the owners are more likely to be involved in the day-to-day running of the business and so they are more likely to display profit-maximising behaviour.

Of course, even in public limited companies, the principal retains a degree of control over the agent. If managers completely ignore profit to focus on alternative objectives they can ultimately be sacked by shareholders. This often leads to behaviour known as *profit satisficing,* where managers aim to produce a satisfactory level of profits needed to keep the shareholders happy and therefore keep them in a job while at the same time pursuing whatever alternative objectives they are motivated by.

Is profit maximisation a sensible assumption to make?

Given the number of alternative objectives firms are sometimes seen to pursue, it is reasonable to question whether profit maximisation is a sensible assumption to make when analysing the behaviour of firms. The reason it remains relevant is that while many of these alternative objectives conflict with profit maximisation in the short run, they can be seen as being consistent with profit maximisation in the long run. For example, while sales or revenue maximising may limit profits in the short run, it may be essential in developing the market share required to maximise profits in the long run. Equally, while a number of firms spend a significant amount of money on corporate social responsibility (CSR) initiatives designed to improve the local community, this can be seen as an important part of developing the reputation of the firm, which again could be important in maximising profits in the long run.

Knowledge check 3

Are small or large firms more likely to pursue alternative maximising objectives?

The relevance of profit maximisation does however ultimately depend upon the nature of the firm being considered. There is no question that a small private firm can be accurately modelled by profit maximisation in both the short run and the long run. For the reasons outlined above, in the case of larger firms profit maximisation is more realistic in the long run than the short run. It is only in the case of public sector and voluntary organisations that there seems no place for the theory of profit maximisation, as even the owners of these firms are not incentivised by profit.

Knowledge check 4
What is likely to be the main objective of public sector and voluntary organisations?

Market structures and their implications for the way resources are allocated and the interdependence of firms

Barriers to entry and exit

Understanding whether there are **barriers to entry** or exit in an industry is crucial in determining which market structure should be used to model firms' behaviour in that industry. Such barriers can take a number of forms:

- *Economies of scale* — if large firms are able to benefit more from significantly lower average costs than small entrants it makes it very difficult for a new firm to enter the market, as they are unable to be price competitive with the incumbent firms.
- *Brand loyalty* — where consumers are loyal to a particular firm it is difficult for a new firm to enter the market, as it will be unable to attract customers even if its product is cheaper or of better quality without spending large amounts on advertising.
- *Legal* — in some cases new firms are unable to enter the market because existing firms have patents in place preventing firms from producing the same product. This is usually to protect intellectual property rights in the case of new inventions.
- *High start-up costs* — new firms will find it difficult to enter an industry that has high fixed costs which need to be paid in order to compete.

Barriers to entry
Obstacles that prevent new firms from entering the market.

Equally, once firms are in the market, there are a number of obstacles they may face that make it difficult for them to leave. Such obstacles are known as barriers to exit. The most common types are:

- *sunk costs* — when there are significant start-up costs that firms could not recover if they were to leave the market (such as advertising expenditure), firms are deterred from exiting because of the losses that would result
- *contracts* — firms may have entered into a number of agreements that prevent them from leaving the market immediately. For example, they may have signed a 1-year lease on premises or they may have made a commitment to supply their product to a particular consumer for a set period of time.

Perfect competition

Assumptions

The following assumptions underpin the model of perfect competition:

- *Short-run profit maximisation* — firms are motivated by achieving the greatest profit possible and therefore produce at the profit-maximising level of output where $MC = MR$.

- *Many buyers and sellers* — there are no dominant firms in the industry, which is instead full of many small firms. This means no firm has the ability to influence the market price and suggests there are no economies of scale to be enjoyed.
- *Homogenous products* — firms produce identical, non-differentiated products. Consumers therefore have no brand loyalty to a particular firm.
- *No barriers to entry or exit* — firms are able to enter the market without cost if they believe it is profitable to do so and can leave without difficulty.
- *Perfect knowledge* — all buyers and sellers have perfect information. Buyers know the prices that all firms in the market are charging and all firms have perfect information about the production methods of other firms.

Exam tip

The assumption of homogenous products is important in the model of perfect competition as it means firms are unable to develop market power through becoming the preferred seller of some consumers.

The demand curve

The fact that no firm has market power means that all firms are price takers — they have to accept whatever price is set by the market as they have no ability to impact the price. This means firms face a perfectly elastic demand curve, as illustrated in Figure 2.

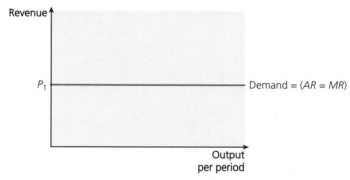

Figure 2 The demand curve in perfect competition

If firms attempted to set a price above P_1, they would lose all of their demand, as all consumers would switch to the many other firms selling the identical product at a price of P_1. Given that the demand curve is perfectly elastic and that a firm's output is small relative to industry output, this means a firm can set as much output as it likes at a price of P_1 — it therefore has no incentive to lower its price to gain more customers as there is unlimited demand at the market price.

Short-run equilibrium

When determining the equilibrium output level and price in theory of the firm analysis, it is important to adhere to the following two rules:

1 Set output where $MC = MR$ — i.e. at the profit-maximising level of output.
2 Set the price at the corresponding point on the demand (AR) curve — i.e. the highest price that can be charged to generate enough demand to purchase the level of output produced.

Figures 3 and 4 illustrate two possible short-run equilibriums. In Figure 3, the firm is making a supernormal profit equal to the size of the shaded region. This is because average revenue exceeds short-run average total costs. In Figure 4, the firm is making a loss, as short-run average total costs exceed average revenue.

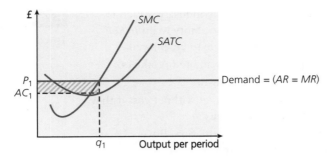

Figure 3 A firm making supernormal profit in the short run

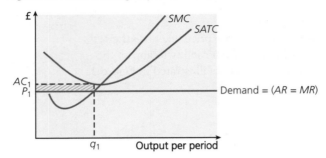

Figure 4 A firm making a loss in the short run

Long-run equilibrium

The fact that no barriers to entry or exit exist in the model of perfect competition means the equilibriums illustrated in Figures 3 and 4 will not exist in the long run. Consider the case of short-run supernormal profits illustrated in Figure 3. New firms will be incentivised to enter the industry to enjoy the supernormal profits being made, causing industry supply to shift to the right from S_1 to S_2 in Figure 5. This causes the price that firms receive to fall from P_1 to P_2. Another way to see this is that each individual firm experiences a lower level of demand for its product (D_2) because there are now more firms in the market. Firms will continue to enter the market until supernormal profit has been eliminated.

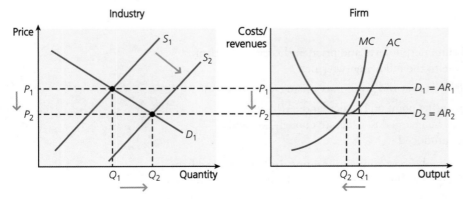

Figure 5 Adjustment to long-run equilibrium

> **Knowledge check 5**
>
> Explain the adjustment that will take place in the long run from the situation illustrated in Figure 4.

This means that in the long run firms in perfect competition will earn only normal profits, as illustrated in Figure 6.

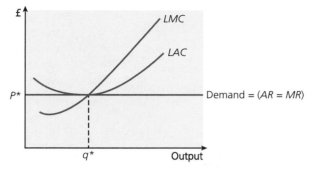

Figure 6 Long-run equilibrium in perfect competition

Efficiency implications

A perfectly competitive firm will be both productively and allocatively efficient. This is because the firm will be operating at the minimum point on its long-run average cost curve (productive efficiency) and price will be equal to marginal cost (allocative efficiency).

However, it is important to note that perfect competition does not necessarily represent the 'perfect' market structure. Many economists have argued supernormal profits are essential to fund research and development, which is essential for generating innovation and long-term quality improvements. Because firms in perfect competition make only normal profits, such firms could be said to be dynamically inefficient, whereby there is a sub-optimal level of investment in research and development to enable long-run improvements in production.

Monopoly

Assumptions

The following assumptions underpin the monopoly model:
- *Short-run profit maximisation* — firms produce at the profit-maximising level of output where $MC = MR$.
- *Single seller of the good* — the industry is dominated by one firm, which is the monopoly seller of the good.
- *No substitutes* — no other firms produce the same or similar products, meaning the monopolist faces no competition.
- *High barriers to entry and exit* — it is difficult for new firms to enter the market, meaning the monopolist is protected from potential competition.

The demand curve

The fact that the monopolist is the only seller of the good makes it a price maker — it is able to influence the price. This is because the output of the firm is equal to the output of the industry, meaning the firm faces a downward-sloping demand curve — the only way to increase output is to reduce the price. The demand (average revenue) curve will be price inelastic as quantity demanded will not be sensitive to changes in price, as there are no close substitutes for consumers to switch from or to when the price changes. This is illustrated in Figure 7. Note that the marginal revenue curve is twice the gradient of the average revenue curve.

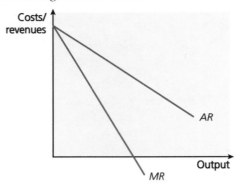

Figure 7 Revenue curves in monopoly

Equilibrium

Following the two standard rules of setting output according to the profit-maximising condition $MC = MR$ and pricing on the demand curve leads to the equilibrium illustrated in Figure 8. A supernormal profit of the shaded region is enjoyed, as average revenue exceeds average cost. Barriers to entry mean that supernormal profits can be sustained in the long run, as potential competitors are unable to enter the market to compete away the supernormal profits.

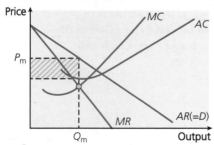

Figure 8 Monopoly equilibrium

Efficiency implications

As illustrated in Figure 8, monopolies are unlikely to be productively or allocatively efficient. The price inelastic demand curve incentivises firms to produce a lower level of output than in perfect competition (as firms know increasing output will result in the price falling), meaning output takes place below the minimum efficient scale and causes productive inefficiency. Moreover, price is significantly above marginal cost, which demonstrates there is allocative inefficiency.

X-inefficiency is also likely to result in the case of a monopoly. Because the firm faces no competitive pressures from other firms, organisational 'slack' is likely to develop. For example, firms may not be motivated to switch input suppliers to reduce costs because they would rather stick with the status quo and feel no pressure to do otherwise. This leads to them operating on an average cost curve above their attainable average cost curve, as illustrated in Figure 9. Firms are experiencing higher average costs not only because they are not operating at the minimum efficient scale

> **Exam tip**
>
> The marginal revenue curve is steeper than the average revenue curve because it reflects the fact that when output increases, the price of all previous units of output has to be decreased to match the new lower price of the final unit of output. The average revenue reflects only the fall in the price of one unit rather than the multiplied impact this has on total revenue in terms of the firm receiving a lower price for its entire quantity of output.

(Q^*) but because they are not achieving their minimum possible average cost at their chosen level of output (C_M instead of C_M^*).

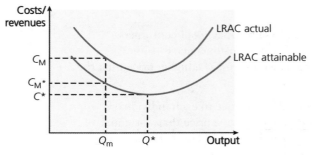

Figure 9 X-inefficiency

There is some debate over whether monopoly firms will be dynamically efficient. Traditional theory argues they have no incentive to invest in research and development because the lack of competition means there is no need to develop their product. However, it is reasonable to suggest there may be a degree of dynamic efficiency in the monopoly model, as firms have supernormal profits which they can use to invest in research and development to improve their product and in doing so increase the barriers to entry, protecting their status as a monopoly firm for years to come.

① Massive cost advantage

Natural monopolies *② Extreme high fixed cost*

While the model of monopoly tends to generate significant inefficiency, there are special circumstances under which it is most efficient for an industry to operate as a monopoly. This occurs when there are substantial economies of scale to be enjoyed, to such an extent that the marginal cost curve remains below the average cost curve over the entire range of output, as illustrated in Figure 10. In these circumstances the incumbent firm is always able to price any potential entrant out of the market because the entrant will face significantly higher average costs since they are operating at a lower scale of output. Economies of scale therefore act as a barrier to entry and create a situation of natural monopoly.

(Central public services)
Natural monoplist
get build pipe big enough to get water across the whole country,
Government regulate
AR = MC (P = MC)
Allocative efficiency

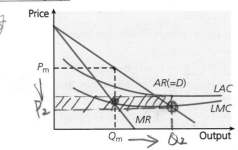

Figure 10 Natural monopoly

Quantity increase hugely $Q_m \to Q_2$
Price fall $P_m \to P_2$.
but natural monopoly make a loss
i) Government subsidise ▨▨ the firm
ii) normal profit made AR = AC

Natural monopolies occur in industries with very high fixed costs and relatively low marginal costs. Utility services are good examples of this. The marginal cost of providing a household with additional water is minimal in comparison with the vast costs involved in setting up a complex network of underground pipes to deliver water to homes. It would be impractical to have multiple firms competing in the water market, all with their own set of extremely expensive pipes, which is why it is sensible for only one company to supply water to every household in a particular area.

Price discrimination

We have assumed until now that firms charge the same price to all consumers. This inevitably means that even in the monopoly case consumers enjoy some consumer surplus — all but the last consumer is willing to pay a higher price than the market price.

However, suppose it were possible to charge a different price to each individual consumer. A monopolist would then charge each consumer a price that was equal to their willingness to pay for the good. The demand curve effectively becomes the marginal revenue curve, as it represents the amount the monopolist will receive for each unit of the good. The impact of this can be illustrated in Figure 11, where for simplicity average and marginal costs are modelled as being constant. While the monopolist's output will increase from Q_m to Q^*, the consumer surplus previously enjoyed will all be transferred to the producer.

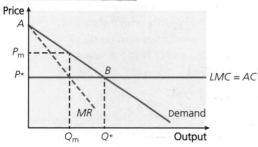

Figure 11 First-degree price discrimination

Such price discrimination is known as first-degree or perfect-price discrimination. While it is rarely possible for firms to charge different prices to each individual consumer, there are several situations in which partial price discrimination exists. For example, swimming pools vary their price according to the age of the individual, with different prices for children, students, adults and pensioners. In order for firms to be able to price discriminate, the following conditions must hold:

- The firm must have market power — price discrimination is possible only when firms are price makers. *monopoly*
- The firm must have information about different consumers — the firm must be able to identify different groups of consumers with different willingness to pay in order to construct a differentiated pricing structure.
- Consumers must have a limited ability to resell the product — if consumers could easily resell the product, the consumers who qualify for lower prices would be able to profit from purchasing the product at the discounted price and selling it at a price just below the higher price to consumers who do not qualify for the discount.

Knowledge check 7

How can railways be seen as an example of a natural monopoly?

Knowledge check 8

Would it be possible for firms in the fast food industry to price discriminate?

Monopolistic competition

Assumptions

The following assumptions underpin the model of monopolistic competition:

- *Short-run profit maximisation* — firms produce at the profit-maximising level of output where $MC = MR$.
- *Many small buyers and sellers* — there are many small firms operating in the industry, none of which has significant market power.
- *No barriers to entry and exit* — new firms are easily able to enter the market if they see supernormal profits are being made and existing firms can leave easily if they are making a loss.
- *Non-homogenous products* — firms produce differentiated products. While there are many substitutes available, none of these is perfect as each firm produces non-identical products, meaning there is a degree of brand loyalty present.

[handwritten margin notes: Slight different products · Maintained by advertising. → Products of other firms are similar, there are some substitute – price elastic, but can be inelastic]

The demand curve

The fact that firms produce differentiated products generates brand loyalty, which means each firm has a degree of market power. Because consumers are not indifferent between firms, a firm will not necessarily lose all of its demand when it increases its price, meaning the demand curve is not perfectly elastic. However, given the large number of relatively close substitutes available, demand is still likely to be relatively elastic, meaning the degree of market power an individual firm has is limited.

Equilibrium

As illustrated in Figure 12, it is possible for a firm operating in a monopolistic competition to make a supernormal profit in the short run, where average revenue exceeds average cost. *[handwritten: AR > AC]*

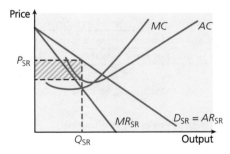

Figure 12 Supernormal profit in monopolistic competition

However, given the freedom of entry and exit in the market, new firms will be attracted by the supernormal profit and will enter the market. This will decrease the demand for existing firms' products and is likely to make the demand curve more price elastic, as there are now a larger number of substitutes available. Entry will continue to occur until supernormal profits are eliminated, resulting in a long-run equilibrium in monopolistic competition where normal profits are made, as illustrated in Figure 13.

> **Exam tip**
>
> It is possible for monopolistically competitive firms to be making a loss in the short run. This will cause some firms to leave the market, increasing the demand for the remaining firms. This process will continue to happen until the long-run equilibrium is reached.

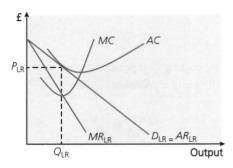

Figure 13 Long-run equilibrium in monopolistic competition

Efficiency implications

Figure 13 demonstrates that firms will be neither productively nor allocatively efficient in the model of monopolistic competition. It could be argued that product differentiation is harming efficiency, as each firm is too small to benefit from economies of scale, with the differentiation giving firms a small amount of pricing power to price above marginal cost. However, this needs to be weighed up against the increased consumer welfare that comes from having more choice.

Firms in this market structure are also less likely to experience X-inefficiency than in monopoly because of the competition they face from other firms. Yet it could be argued that the money firms spend on differentiating their products (perhaps through advertising) leads to them experiencing higher average costs than they need otherwise have, generating an element of X-inefficiency.

Oligopoly

Assumptions

- *High 3–5 firm concentration ratio* — the industry is dominated by a few large firms which account for a significant proportion of market share. There may be a large number of firms in the industry, but there are a few firms that have significant market power.
- *Short-run profit maximisers* — firms produce at the profit-maximising level of output where $MC = MR$.
- *High barriers to entry and exit* — it is difficult for new firms to enter the market, meaning the dominant firms are protected from potential competition.
- *Firms are interdependent* — the actions of one firm impact upon the other firms in the industry.

Kinked demand curve

The model of oligopoly is founded on kinked demand curve theory, which centres on the fact that there is an asymmetric response by firms to changes in another firm's price. Suppose a firm is considering changing its price from P^*, as illustrated in Figure 14.

> **n-firm concentration ratio** A measure of the market share of the largest n firms in an industry.

If the firm decides to increase its price, other firms will keep their prices unchanged, seizing the opportunity to steal some market share. This will cause the firm that has raised its price to experience a significant decrease in demand, as the majority of consumers will switch away to the firms that have kept their price unchanged. This means the demand curve is price elastic above a price of P^*. However, if the firm chooses to lower its price, other firms will respond by lowering their prices in order to avoid losing market share. This means the firm that initially lowered its price will experience hardly any increase in its demand, as it will not steal customers from other firms. Thus the demand curve is price inelastic below a price of P^*. This generates a discontinuous marginal revenue curve, reflecting the fact that the nature of this market means there can be sudden jumps in total revenue as a result of small changes in price.

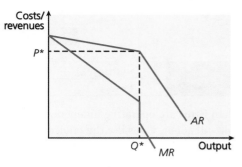

Figure 14 Kinked demand curve

Behaviour of firms

Kinked demand curve theory gives rise to a number of important insights, which explain the behaviour of firms in an oligopoly:

- *Price wars* — because firms are making supernormal profits, they are incentivised to lower their prices to steal market share and make even greater profits. However, when one firm does this, other firms react, causing prices to fall rapidly to a new equilibrium. Providing the new equilibrium occurs at a level where supernormal profits are still being made, though, firms will continue to have an incentive to engage in further price wars.

- *Price rigidity* — given that firms will lose revenue if they decide to either increase or decrease their prices (because of the nature of the kinked demand curve), prices are likely to be stable in the model of oligopoly. Figure 15 illustrates that even when there is an increase in costs, prices might well remain constant in order to avoid disturbing the equilibrium that has been established.

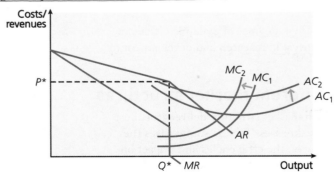

Figure 15 Price rigidity in oligopoly

- *Collusion* — to avoid price wars, firms have the incentive to collude (work together to maximise their joint profits). This can be illustrated by the simple Prisoner's Dilemma set out in Table 1. Firms A and B have a choice between pricing low and high. The potential revenues available to Firm A are shown by the figures on the left-hand side of each pair, with the revenues available to Firm B shown on the right-hand side.

> **Exam tip**
>
> If costs increased enough to shift the marginal cost curve above the discontinuous part of the marginal revenue curve then the oligopolist would be forced to increase prices. However, providing the increase in costs remains relatively small, the equilibrium will be undisturbed.

Table 1

		Firm B	
		High	**Low**
Firm A	**High**	£10m, £10m	£1m, £15m
	Low	£15m, £1m	£5m, £5m

When firms are operating independently they do not know which strategy the other firm will adopt. Consider the choice facing Firm A. If Firm B prices 'High', Firm A should price 'Low' (£15m is better than £10m). If Firm B prices 'Low', Firm A should price 'Low' (£5m is better than £1m). Therefore, regardless of what Firm B does, the best response for Firm A is to price 'Low'. The same logic can be used to explain why Firm B will also decide to price 'Low'. Each firm will earn a profit of £5m — well below the £10m they could earn if they colluded, agreeing to both price 'High'.

Firms may decide to enter a cartel to achieve this, where they reach an agreement on price and output in order to maximise their joint profits. In practice, however, cartels are illegal. Tacit collusion is therefore a strategy that firms are more likely to adopt.

Price leadership is a good example of this, where one firm (perhaps the most established) sets prices and other firms are happy to follow these prices, knowing that doing so will maximise joint profits and avoid price wars.

■ *Non-price competition* — given that firms do not tend to compete on price, oligopoly is characterised by significant non-price competition. Vast amounts of money are spent on developing brand loyalty and emphasising the quality of the product in order for firms to attract customers from other firms charging the same price as them.

> **Tacit collusion** A situation occurring when firms refrain from competing on price, but without communication or formal agreement between them.

Efficiency implications

Figure 15 illustrates that firms in oligopoly will be neither productively nor allocatively efficient. The downward-sloping demand curve means firms are incentivised to restrict output below the minimum efficient scale and through collusion prices will be kept above marginal cost.

The non-price competition is likely to result in high degrees of dynamic efficiency, with firms using their supernormal profits to invest in research and development to improve the quality of their product.

Comparing the outcomes of different market structures

It is difficult to reach a conclusion about which market structure delivers the 'best' outcome, as each has its own strengths and weaknesses. Table 2 summarises the features of the four market structures, focusing on the efficiencies and impact on consumer welfare (measured by price, choice and quality). The question marks indicate situations in which there are strong arguments on both sides about whether the feature is present in the market structure.

Table 2

	Perfect competition	Monopolistic competition	Oligopoly	Monopoly
Allocative efficiency	✓	✗	✗	✗
Productive efficiency	✓	✗	✗	✗
Dynamic efficiency	?	✓	✗	?
X-efficiency	✓	✓	✓	✗
Low prices	✓	✗	✗	?
Wide choice	✗	✓	?	✗
High quality	?	✓	✓	?

Knowledge check 9

What arguments could be made to justify the suggestion that better outcomes are achieved for consumers in the monopoly market structure than in the monopolistically competitive market structure?

Alternative theories of firms' behaviour

In order to reduce the risk of supernormal profits being competed away firms may engage in pricing strategies that differ from those suggested by the theory of profit maximisation — these are known as predatory pricing and limit pricing.

Predatory pricing

Predatory pricing is an anti-competitive strategy where a firm sets its price below average variable cost in an attempt to force rivals out of business. Suppose a new firm enters a market and attempts to steal market share from an established firm which is enjoying supernormal profits by setting a price that is lower than that charged by the established firm. In order to return to a situation in which it faces no competition and so can charge high prices again, the established firm may choose to significantly reduce its price in the short run, knowing it is likely to be able to sustain a loss for a longer period than the entrant because it has greater financial reserves. The hope is that this will force the entrant out of the market, at which point the established firm can increase the price to the previous level.

This practice is illegal in the EU because it is clear that the only motive firms could have for operating when their price is below average variable cost is to drive other firms out of business. While predatory pricing could be seen at first glance to be beneficial to consumers because of the low prices it brings, this is of course only a short-term gain — in the long term, consumers are likely to suffer from higher prices and decreased choice as a result of this strategy. However, in practice it is very difficult for courts to prove that firms are engaging in predatory pricing as opposed to standard competitive practices. Moreover, established firms might not even have to lower their prices to prevent entry — if a potential entrant knows the established firm has the ability to predatory price they will be disincentivised from entering the market in the first place.

⚙ Limit pricing

Knowing that it is high levels of supernormal profits that attract entrants, an incumbent firm may decide to set a price below the profit-maximising level, limiting its supernormal profits in the short run but ensuring it does not get driven down to making only normal profits in the long run as a result of another firm entering the market.

Exam tip

Predatory pricing will not necessarily lead to the new firm going out of business; providing it has the funds available to survive making a loss in the short run, it may remain in the market knowing the incumbent's actions are unsustainable.

Economies of scale mean incumbent firms are likely to have natural cost advantages over an entrant. When high levels of supernormal profit are being made the entrant is not deterred by this, as they know it is possible for them to price below the incumbent firm and still make a normal profit, even with their higher costs. However, when the incumbent firm engages in limit pricing, its lower costs mean it can continue making a supernormal profit while pricing below a level an entrant would be able to charge at to achieve a normal profit. This will therefore disincentivise new firms from entering the market.

Contestable markets

William Baumol's theory of contestable markets demonstrates how a dominant firm may behave competitively because of the potential competition it faces. For a market to be contestable, there must be no barriers to entry or exit or sunk costs — that is, a firm must be able to recover all costs associated with setting up in the industry. All firms must also have access to the same technology, resulting in no one firm having a cost advantage over another firm.

In such a market, there is a threat of hit-and-run competition. Because of the ease of entry and exit, it is possible for a firm outside of the market to observe supernormal profits being made, enter the market and then leave it again having taken some of the supernormal profit.

Under these circumstances firms are unable to charge a price above average cost. The impact of this on a monopolist can be seen in Figure 16, with the price decreasing and output decreasing compared with the standard monopoly outcome. Note that despite a monopolist facing no actual competition, they are forced to behave competitively because of the potential competition they face.

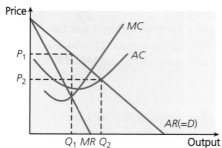

Figure 16 Contestable market

This clearly moves the market closer to an allocatively and productively efficient outcome and delivers beneficial outcomes for consumers. In fact, a perfectly contestable market will result in both productive and allocative efficiency being achieved in the long run, as firms operating at any point other than at the bottom of their average cost curve will incentivise new firms to enter the market to enjoy supernormal profits.

Growth of firms

A striking feature of the economy today is the way in which it is increasingly dominated by large firms. Such firms are incentivised to increase their scale of output in order to gain market power within an industry; doing so will enable them to have

| Knowledge check 10 |

In the real world, it is unlikely that many monopolists are operating in contestable markets. Why is this?

some pricing power and could potentially enable supernormal profits to be made. In a globalised world in which many firms face significant international competition, there is also a need for firms to grow in order to benefit from economies of scale and remain price competitive.

Growth can be categorised into internal (organic) and external (mergers and acquisitions) growth:

■ *Organic growth* — if a firm is successful in attracting new customers, perhaps as a result of an effective marketing campaign, it may be able to achieve internal growth. easyJet, for example, developed its market power in this way, through gradually purchasing more planes and increasing the number of flights it operated. However, once firms have exhausted any growth they can enjoy from taking market share from their competitors, they may look to diversify to experience further **organic growth**, expanding the product range to enable more increases in output.

■ *Mergers and acquisitions* — a firm may choose to expand through merging with another firm, combining resources to become a single entity. The merger of T-Mobile and Orange is a recent example of this, when the companies merged to form the new entity EE. Alternatively, a firm may take over another firm — this is known as an acquisition.

Types of integration

■ *Horizontal integration* — this is when a firm merges with another firm in the same industry at the same stage of the production process. The merger of T-Mobile and Orange is an example of horizontal integration. This type of integration enables firms to develop market power by reducing the level of competition in the market.

■ *Vertical integration* — this is when a firm merges with another firm in the same industry at a different stage of the production process. Merging with a firm at an earlier stage of the production process is known as backward vertical integration — an example of this would be if a grocery store acquired a farm. Merging with a firm at a later stage of the production process is known as forward vertical integration — a car manufacturer acquiring a car sales dealership would be an example of this. Engaging in vertical integration means firms are less reliant on other firms in the production process.

■ *Conglomerate integration* — this is when a firm merges with another firm operating in a different industry, such as a fast-food firm acquiring a clothes-manufacturing business. While such integration enables a firm to spread its risk (if one industry suffers the firm is still able to enjoy the growth of another industry), it can harm a firm's efficiency because the different industries may require very different management techniques and operational procedures.

Evaluating integration

While external growth tends to be more expensive than internal growth, it is attractive to firms because it enables them to expand their output much more quickly than organic growth would allow. Moreover, mergers and acquisitions provide an immediate opportunity to enjoy cost savings through rationalisation — for example, the new larger firm does not need to have two head offices so can close one and spread the cost of the remaining one over a larger scale of output.

However, not all mergers result in the success firms were hoping to achieve. This is because firms can run into unexpected integration problems, such as finding two

Organic growth
Expansion of a firm's operations using its own resources.

Knowledge check 11

Suppose a lightbulb manufacturer acquired a DIY store. What type of integration would this represent?

different production systems difficult to combine. Differences in the culture of the two firms can also mean productivity gains are not as substantial as hoped for.

Regulation

When firms grow too big and develop market power, consumers are likely to suffer from reduced choice and higher prices. In cases where potential competition does not exist because of significant barriers to entry, governments often choose to intervene in order to protect consumer welfare. The Competition and Markets Authority (CMA) exists to investigate markets in which competition appears to be weak and it has the power to make rulings designed to protect consumer welfare. It is likely to investigate any market in which firms have more than 25% market share.

An example of this came in the 2007 investigation of the British Aviation Authority (BAA) by the Competition Commission (which has since been replaced by the CMA). The Competition Commission ruled that the dominance BAA had over the airport market in the southeast of England (BAA owned Heathrow, Gatwick and Stansted airports) was not in the best interest of consumers and forced the company to sell off two of its three London airports. As a result, Gatwick airport was sold in 2009, with Stansted airport being sold in 2013.

Deciding when to intervene to achieve the best outcome for consumers is far from straightforward. While a firm may have in excess of 25% market share, the CMA may decide that the productive efficiency that this scale enables the firm to achieve ultimately benefits consumers. Moreover, establishing whether a firm is abusing its market power in increasing its price is difficult, as such action cannot be isolated from inevitable fluctuations in market conditions which would cause the price to rise even in a competitive market.

> **Knowledge check 12**
>
> Would the CMA intervene to reduce the market power held by a firm in the case of a natural monopoly?

Summary

After studying the topic of *Competition and market power* you should be able to:

- Evaluate the different objectives a firm may pursue and explain the factors that influence the choice of objectives.
- Explain why firms will profit maximise when $MC = MR$.
- Analyse the different types of barriers to entry and exit that may be present in a market.
- Explain, with the aid of a diagram, the model of perfect competition in the short run and the long run.
- Explain, with the aid of a diagram, the model of monopoly.
- Evaluate the implications of the existence of a natural monopoly.
- Explain, with the aid of a diagram, the model of monopolistic competition in the short run and the long run.

- Explain, with the aid of a diagram, the model of oligopoly, understanding the notion of the kinked demand curve and the role collusion plays in oligopolistic markets.
- Compare and contrast the outcomes of perfect competition, monopolistic competition, oligopoly and monopoly, including the implications on efficiency and consumer welfare.
- Understand what is meant by predatory pricing and limit pricing as alternative pricing strategies to profit maximisation.
- Evaluate, with a diagram, the advantages and disadvantages of a perfectly contestable market.
- Analyse the different types of economic integration and evaluate the advantages and disadvantages of integration to economic agents.
- Evaluate the impact of competition policy on the behaviour of firms.

Labour market

Wage determination

Demand for labour

The most crucial element of labour demand to understand is that labour is not demanded for its own sake but for the revenue that it can generate for firms. This makes labour a derived demand — demand for labour is dependent on the demand for the output that it produces.

In practice, 'the' labour market actually consists of a number of sub-markets, all of which are in some senses interrelated but in others operate independently of each other. The nature of labour demand varies in all of these sub-markets — for example, both the level and type of labour demanded in Bristol for engineers will be different from the labour demanded in Newcastle for hairdressers.

Given that labour is demanded for the revenue it generates for firms, labour demand can be modelled by the marginal revenue product of labour (MRP_L):

$$MRP_L = MPP_L \times MR$$

The marginal physical product of labour (MPP_L) represents the change in total output as a result of employing one additional worker. The marginal revenue (MR) represents the change in total revenue as a result of selling one more unit of output. Assuming the labour market is perfectly competitive and marginal revenue is therefore perfectly elastic, this therefore means MR is effectively equal to the price of the product.

This means that labour demand will be high when workers produce a large volume of output (MPP_L is high) and each unit of that output is very valuable (MR is high). The MRP_L curve is downward sloping because the law of diminishing returns demonstrates that the additional output produced by each additional unit of labour is expected to fall, as *ceteris paribus* the same stock of capital has to be shared between more workers.

Figure 17 illustrates how the profit-maximising level of employment is determined — where the marginal revenue product of labour is equal to the marginal cost of labour (MC_L). This can be explained by ruling out the only other possible positions:

- When $MRP_L > MC_L$, the change in total revenue derived from employing an additional worker exceeds the change in total cost. Firms can therefore make a greater profit by employing more workers, meaning this is not the profit-maximising level of employment.
- When $MC_L > MRP_L$, the change in total cost from employing an additional worker exceeds the change in total revenue. Firms can therefore make a greater profit by employing fewer workers, meaning this is not the profit-maximising level of employment.

This means the profit-maximising level of employment must occur when the change in total revenue from employing an additional worker equals the change in total cost — that is, when $MRP_L = MC_L$.

Knowledge check 13

Explain what would happen to the demand for labour if there was an increase in workers' productivity.

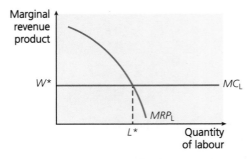

Figure 17 Profit-maximising level of employment

Wage elasticity of demand for labour

The **wage elasticity of demand for labour** measures how sensitive a firm's demand for labour is in response to a change in the wage rate. It is determined by a number of factors:

■ *Ease of factor substitution* — when labour can be easily substituted for capital, demand will be wage elastic, as a small increase in the wage rate will cause firms to swap labour for capital. While technological progress is increasing the number of situations in which labour can be swapped for capital, in instances where labour is essential demand tends to be wage inelastic (pilots are a good example of this).

■ *Share of labour costs in firm's total costs* — when labour costs account for a high proportion of total costs, demand tends to be wage inelastic, as small changes in the wage have a significant impact on the profitability of the firm.

■ *Time period* — in the short run, demand for labour is often wage inelastic, as even when wages increase firms are not easily able to substitute labour for capital. In the long run, labour demand becomes more wage elastic as firms can respond to the change in the wage rate (for example, in the long run firms can replace checkout assistants with self-service checkout machines, which cannot be done overnight as it takes time to purchase and install such machines).

■ *Price elasticity of demand for the product* — when demand for the product is price inelastic, demand for labour is likely to be wage inelastic, as any increases in the wage rate can simply be passed on to consumers in the form of higher prices. When demand for the product is price elastic, an increase in wages and the subsequent increase in price will lead to a significant reduction in the demand for the product, causing the derived demand for labour to fall and respond more than proportionally to a change in the wage rate.

Supply of labour

Individual labour supply

In determining how an individual responds to an increase in the wage rate, it is important to understand the two conflicting effects influencing their behaviour:

■ *Substitution effect* — the opportunity cost of leisure is the income that could have been earned from working. Therefore, when wages increase, the opportunity cost of leisure time increases, incentivising individuals to substitute leisure for work in order to enjoy the higher wages on offer. The substitution effect therefore encourages individuals to work more hours when the wage rate increases.

> **Wage elasticity of demand for labour** Responsiveness of quantity of labour demanded to a change in the wage rate.

> **Knowledge check 14**
>
> On the same diagram, draw a wage-elastic and wage-inelastic demand for labour curve.

■ *Income effect* — leisure is a normal good. When the wage rate increases, individuals have more income and therefore demand more leisure. The income effect therefore encourages individuals to work fewer hours when the wage rate increases.

Which effect dominates depends on the wage rate, as illustrated in Figure 18. At low wages (below W^*) the substitution effect dominates — extra income can make a significant difference to an individual's standard of living (large substitution effect), while the income effect is small because at low wages individuals cannot afford good-quality leisure time (small income effect). This means individuals will work more hours when the wage rate increases at low wages. At high wages (above W^*) the income effect dominates — at high levels of income individuals can afford high-quality leisure so really value additional leisure time (large income effect) and do not value additional income as they already have sufficient to afford the goods and services they desire (small substitution effect). This means individuals will work fewer hours when the wage rate increases at high wages, generating a backward-bending labour supply curve.

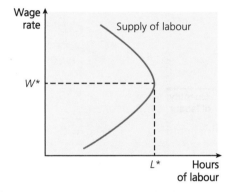

Figure 18 Backward-bending individual labour supply curve

While this approach offers a sensible theoretical framework through which to explain individual labour supply, it is unlikely to be particularly relevant in real-world labour markets. This is because in practice most individuals are appointed on a fixed-hours contract and rarely get the opportunity to vary their hours of work according to changes in the wage rate.

Industry labour supply

At an industry level where firms have the choice of either increasing the working hours of existing employees or hiring new workers from other industries, the labour supply curve is upward sloping — an increase in the wage rate will either incentivise existing workers to work longer hours or new workers to supply their labour to the industry.

While wage is clearly a crucial determinant of labour supply, there are a number of other factors that influence the supply of labour to a profession. These include:

■ *pecuniary (financial) non-wage benefits* — labour supply may be greater at every given wage rate (at S_B in Figure 19) in industries where there is an opportunity to earn overtime pay or commission

Exam tip

It is important to remember that the individual labour supply curve is personal to the individual — the slope of the curve and the level of W^* will depend on the relative importance placed on leisure and income.

- *job security* — individuals may be willing to accept a lower wage if the chances of them losing their job are slim
- *holiday entitlement* — labour supply is likely to be higher in industries that offer workers generous holiday entitlement
- *working conditions* — labour supply is likely to be relatively low (at S_A in Figure 19) in comparison with other professions offering similar wages when the work is unpleasant (e.g. sewage cleaners) or when the job requires individuals to work unsociable hours (e.g. care home workers)
- *fringe benefits* — some employers offer workers incentives such as a company car or private health insurance. Labour supply is likely to be relatively high in such industries.

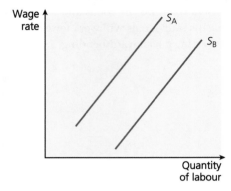

Figure 19 Differences in labour supply

Wage elasticity of supply of labour

The **wage elasticity of supply of labour** measures the extent to which an increase in the wage rate will encourage an increase in the supply of labour to an occupation. It is determined by a number of factors:

- *Qualifications and skills* — labour supply is likely to be inelastic in occupations that require a high degree of qualifications and skills, as when the wage rate increases few individuals who are not already in it have the necessary attributes required to enter the occupation.
- *Length of training* — labour supply will be more elastic when little training is required to enter the profession, as when the wage rate increases individuals are easily able to switch into the occupation and supply their labour.
- *Mobility of labour* — when there is a significant amount of geographical immobility, labour supply is likely to be inelastic. This is because when the wage rate to an occupation increases, labour supply will increase less than proportionally as many individuals will be unwilling to relocate in order to supply their labour, perhaps because of family ties or regional house price differentials.
- *Time period* — labour supply will become more elastic in the long run, as individuals tend to become more occupationally and geographically mobile over time (they can, for example, study for the qualifications to enter professions with rising wages).

Knowledge check 15

How might the recent performance of a firm affect whether an individual chooses to supply their labour to that firm?

Wage elasticity of supply of labour Responsiveness of quantity of labour supplied to a change in the wage rate.

Knowledge check 16

On the same diagram, draw a wage-elastic and wage-inelastic supply of labour curve.

Labour market equilibrium

Labour market equilibrium occurs when the supply of labour is equal to the demand for labour, as illustrated in Figure 20.

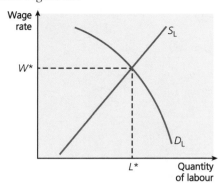

Figure 20 Labour market equilibrium

If the wage rate was below W^* there would be excess demand for labour, meaning firms would have to increase the wage rate in order to incentivise the extension along the supply curve needed to fill their vacancies. If the wage rate was above W^* there would be excess supply of labour, putting downward pressure on wages until the equilibrium was reached.

Changes in any of the factors determining the supply or demand of labour will cause the equilibrium wage rate and employment level to change. For example, suppose improved education and training raised workers' skill levels, increasing productivity and therefore the marginal physical product of labour. This would cause the marginal revenue product of labour to increase and, as workers could now generate more revenue for firms, such workers would now become more desirable and the demand curve for labour would shift to the right, as illustrated in Figure 21. This would cause the equilibrium wage rate to increase from W_0 to W_1 and the quantity of labour employed to increase from L_0 to L_1.

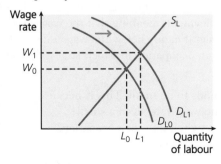

Figure 21 Changes in the labour market equilibrium

Transfer earnings and economic rent

When an individual decides to supply their labour to a particular occupation, the opportunity cost is the sacrifice of the wage they could have earned in another occupation (their **transfer earnings**). Assuming *ceteris paribus*, if individuals are

Transfer earnings The minimum payment required to keep a factor of production in its present use.

behaving rationally they will supply their labour to an occupation only when the wage is at least equal to their transfer earnings — if the wage were any lower than this individuals would supply their labour to an alternative occupation. This means transfer earnings can be represented by the area under the supply curve up to the equilibrium employment level, as illustrated in Figure 22.

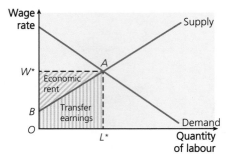

Figure 22 Transfer earnings and economic rent

Given that in any one occupation workers doing the same job are likely to have different levels of transfer earnings (some individuals will have better outside options than others) but earn the same wage rate, it is inevitable that some workers will therefore enjoy a surplus payment above their transfer earnings — this surplus is known as **economic rent**. This is illustrated by the area above the supply curve and below the wage rate in Figure 22.

The proportion of the wage that is accounted for by economic rent is primarily determined by the wage elasticity of supply of labour. When labour supply is highly inelastic, wages need to be increased by a large amount to incentivise even a small increase in quantity of labour supplied, often because few individuals have the skills or qualifications required to supply their labour to that industry. In such professions economic rent tends to be large, with transfer earnings accounting for a low proportion of the wage. This can be explained by the fact that a fall in the wage rate would not cause a significant fall in the quantity of labour supplied, as workers are likely to have invested significant time training in the profession or have specialist skills that would not be useful in another form of employment, meaning that the wage rate in the next best alternative occupation would be significantly below the wage rate they currently receive. Doctors are a good example of an occupation in which large economic rent is enjoyed.

When the supply of labour is elastic, economic rent tends to be small. This is because given the sensitivity of labour supply to a change in the wage rate, even a small amount of economic rent would incentivise workers to switch into the occupation. Moreover, given skills and qualifications are likely to be less specialist in such occupations, individuals are likely to be able to move to another occupation and earn a similar wage to what they are currently earning, meaning transfer earnings are close to the current wage rate. Waitressing is a good example of an occupation in which transfer earnings account for a large proportion of the wage.

Economic rent
A payment received by a factor of production over and above what would be needed to keep it in its present use.

Exam tip

The level of demand is also important in explaining how much economic rent workers enjoy — when MRP_L is high, workers are very valuable to firms and will be paid a high wage rate which, when combined with an inelastic supply of labour, will mean economic rent is likely to be high.

The impact of market power on wage determination

Trade unions

Trade unions are organisations of workers that negotiate with employers on behalf of their members. Such negotiations are designed to achieve higher wages, improved working conditions and greater job security.

A powerful union is effectively able to act as the monopoly supplier of labour to an industry. Suppose members of a union refuse to supply their labour below a wage of W^*, as illustrated in Figure 23.

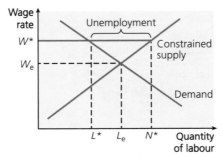

Figure 23 Trade union wage bargaining

The supply of labour is effectively constrained — firms are now unable to employ any workers below the union's target wage rate. Note that while firms cannot pay a wage below W^*, there is nothing to stop them paying a wage above this, which is why the new labour supply curve is not entirely elastic, as firms will need to pay a wage above W^* if they want to employ more than N^* workers.

In these circumstances the trade union will be successful in achieving an increase in the wage rate from W_e to W^*. However, this comes at a cost of reduced employment, with $(L_e - L^*)$ workers losing their jobs because of the contraction along the labour demand curve. As the increase in the wage rate also incentivises $(N^* - L_e)$ additional workers to enter the labour market, further unemployment is generated by the union bargaining. The amount of unemployment created will be particularly large when labour demand is elastic, as pushing up the wage rate will result in a significant contraction along the labour demand curve.

The union has caused labour market failure of unemployment and resulted in the wage rate being above the competitive equilibrium. In instances where unions are able to negotiate improved job security for their members they are likely to contribute to further labour market failure in the form of reducing labour market flexibility, as firms now find it more difficult to adjust the number of workers they employ in response to changes in consumer demand.

However, it is not necessarily the case that union intervention will inevitably cause labour market failure in competitive labour markets. In an increasingly globalised world in which firms face fierce international competition, many unions have recognised that the traditional approach to wage bargaining is no longer effective, as it could well result in firms relocating production abroad, replacing workers with capital or going out of business because of the damage caused to price competitiveness.

Exam tip

Bargaining for improved job security for workers will not necessarily cause labour market failure. If it results in workers feeling more motivated and as a consequence being more productive, this could in fact benefit the efficiency of a firm.

Therefore, many unions work with firms to increase workers' productivity, for example by offering training courses. This raises the marginal revenue product of labour and subsequently causes the labour demand curve to shift to the right, as shown in Figure 24. This causes the equilibrium wage rate to rise from W_1 to W_2, generating the higher wages desired by union members without damaging employment levels.

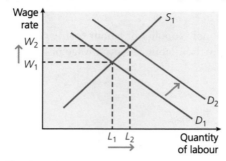

Figure 24 Trade unions contributing to improved productivity

Monopsony

In competitive labour markets no one firm is able to influence the wage rate — because each firm employs a small number of workers relative to the size of the industry's labour market, firms are able to employ more workers by simply paying the going wage rate.

A monopsony firm is the single buyer of labour in an industry. This means it faces the industry labour supply curve directly as it is a wage maker — the only way to increase the number of workers employed is to increase the wage rate, as represented by the upward-sloping supply curve in Figure 25.

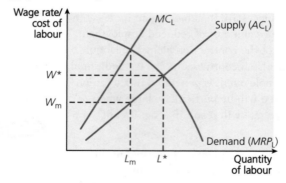

Figure 25 Monopsony

The marginal cost of labour exceeds the average cost of labour as when the firm chooses to hire an extra worker it not only has to pay that worker's wage (the AC_L) but also has to raise the wage paid to all the other workers employed. This makes hiring additional workers particularly costly in the model of monopsony.

Monopsonists will set employment according to the profit-maximising condition $MC_L = MRP_L$. If $MC_L > MRP_L$ the change in total cost as a result of employing the last worker would be greater than the change in total revenue derived from employing the last worker, meaning a larger profit could be made by employing fewer workers.

If $MRP_L > MC_L$ the change in total revenue as a result of employing one more worker would be greater than the change in total cost as a result of employing one more worker, meaning a larger profit could be made by employing more workers. This explains why employment will be where $MC_L = MRP_L$ at L_m. Firms will then pay the wage rate on the corresponding point of the labour supply curve, as W_m is the wage needed to attract L_m workers to supply their labour.

As the wage rate is below the competitive equilibrium wage rate W^*, monopsonies cause labour market failure. They are able to exploit their market power to pay workers below their marginal revenue product, knowing that they are the sole buyer of labour so there is no threat of workers leaving to work for a rival firm paying higher wages. Moreover, the quantity of labour employed is below the competitive equilibrium of L^*, meaning monopsonies create a labour market failure of unemployment. This is because the firm finds hiring additional workers so costly that it chooses to restrict the number of workers it employs as this allows it to pay low wages (employing more workers would force the firm to raise the wage rate of all workers).

Bilateral monopoly

The analysis of monopsony so far assumes that the monopsonist holds all the market power in wage negotiations. Consider now a situation of bilateral monopoly — when there is a monopoly seller of labour (a trade union) to negotiate wages with a monopoly buyer of labour (a monopsonist). Acting as a monopoly supplier of labour, the union can take away the wage-making power of the monopsony by refusing to supply labour below a target wage rate. Suppose this target wage rate is at W_{TU} in Figure 26. This will not only result in the wage rate moving closer to the competitive equilibrium but will also increase the quantity of labour employed to L_{TU} – the monopsony employs more workers because it has less incentive to restrict employment as even if it hired L_M workers it would still have to pay the union's target wage of W_{TU}. In fact, the union is able to target any wage increase up to W_{MAX} without experiencing any adverse employment consequences in comparison with the monopsony outcome. In the case of bilateral monopoly, then, trade unions can be seen to help correct rather than cause labour market failure.

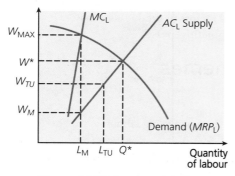

Figure 26 Bilateral monopoly

The outcome achieved will depend on the relative bargaining power of the trade union. When demand for labour is inelastic, unions are likely to be more successful in bargaining for a higher wage — there is little risk of firms replacing workers for capital, meaning they are more likely to give in to the union's wage demands, and the price elasticity of demand for the product may be inelastic, meaning firms can simply pass on the higher wage costs to consumers. When demand for labour is elastic, unions are unlikely to be able to achieve a wage much above the monopsony wage of W_M — the firm could, for example, simply be able to outsource production if unions attempted to bargain for high wages.

Unit labour costs

Unit labour costs measure the labour costs per unit of output. They can be calculated by:

Labour costs ÷ Output per worker

Labour costs include all costs associated with employing workers, including wages, tax and pension contributions, maternity leave and training costs. Output per worker is a measure of labour productivity.

Unit labour costs are an important determinant of international competitiveness. When one country has higher unit labour costs than another country it is likely to worsen the price competitiveness of the goods and services produced in that country, thus worsening the balance of payments.

The UK suffers from relatively high unit labour costs in comparison with other EU nations and the USA. There are two primary explanations for this:

■ *Relatively high labour costs* — the UK is one of the richest countries in the EU with a relatively high minimum wage. Employing workers is therefore more expensive in the UK than in many other nations.
■ *Relatively poor labour productivity* — strong employment protection laws in the UK in comparison with countries such as the USA mean workers are less productive as they experience greater job security and are therefore potentially more likely to slack.

However, having high unit labour costs may not be as damaging to firms as it might at first appear. This is because price is not the only factor on which firms compete — if a firm is producing a high-quality good then it may not matter that unit labour costs are relatively high. Moreover, a country's goods and services may even be internationally price competitive despite high unit labour costs if production is capital intensive or uses more efficient capital than other countries. Therefore, total factor productivity (total output divided by total input of all factors of production) may perhaps be a better way to measure international competitiveness.

Labour market issues and themes

Labour market data

There are some important terms you need to know when analysing labour market data:

■ *Working-age population* — all individuals aged between 16 and 64. Note that as the state retirement age increases beyond 65 over the coming years the upper limit will increase beyond 64.
■ *Dependency ratio* — ratio of those aged 15 or below and 65 and above to the working population. In the UK approximately 21 million people are aged 15 and below or 65 and above and approximately 36.5 million people are of working age, giving a dependency ratio of 0.58 (36.5m divided by 36.5m + 21m).

> **Exam tip**
>
> It is important to understand which measure of labour productivity is being used when making international comparisons. For example, when measured by output per worker the UK has relatively high labour productivity in comparison with countries like Italy and Spain, but this is because working hours are longer in the UK — measuring labour productivity as output per worker per hour would yield a different result.

- *Labour force* — number of people of working age who are either employed or unemployed, sometimes referred to as the economically active population.
- *Participation rate* — the proportion of the working-age population that is economically active (i.e. is in the labour force).
- *Economically inactive* — number of people of working age who are not participating in the labour market. Students, home-makers, the disabled and the early-retired are all examples of groups of individuals that fall into this category.
- *International Labour Organization (ILO) unemployment rate* — measures the percentage of the labour force that is unemployed, defined as those who are available for and actively seeking work but are without a job.

The nature of employment has changed dramatically due to structural change in the economy. Between 1990 and 2014 the proportion of jobs accounted for by the manufacturing sector fell from 18% to 8% while the proportion of jobs accounted for by the service sector increased from 73% to 85%.

Knowledge check 17

Which factors have contributed to the deindustrialisation of the UK economy?

Discrimination

The existence of wage differentials between different groups in society suggests some discrimination may be present in the labour market. For example, there is a narrowing but persistent gender pay gap, which sees women earn less than men, and evidence of poor employment opportunities for some ethnic minority groups. It is important, though, to recognise that inequality between different groups does not necessarily prove discrimination is taking place, as economic theory may explain such inequality in part. For example, we know that differences in education and training significantly affect the marginal revenue product of labour and thus wages — it is therefore not surprising that there is a correlation between the educational attainment of ethnic groups and the wages they receive. Moreover, the gender pay gap can be partially explained by childcare responsibilities, which often interrupt the working life of women, causing them to take time out of the labour market or choose to supply their labour part time.

Despite this, however, labour market economists agree wage differentials must be explained in part by discrimination. There are a number of theories that have been proposed to model discrimination, including:

- *Becker's taste-based discrimination theory* — Becker argued wages are determined by the net advantages of employing a particular worker, in terms of both the profit they can bring the firm and the non-monetary benefits they bring. Therefore, employers will *ceteris paribus* pay workers they like working with a higher wage.
- *Statistical discrimination* — employers have imperfect information as to which workers are productive (workers) and which workers aren't (shirkers). They therefore use generalised information to discriminate against certain workers — they know on average that workers from certain groups are less productive than others and because they cannot test this in specific cases they set wages according to the general evidence.

Labour market flexibility

Flexibility in the labour market is crucial to the performance of an economy. Consumer demand and comparative advantage are constantly changing, and the labour market needs to be able to adapt to such changes in order to allow resources to be allocated efficiently and for international competitiveness to be maintained.

A flexible labour market is characterised by workers being able to easily switch between jobs or between occupations. A crucial barrier to flexibility is immobility, which can come in two forms: geographical or occupational.

Geographical immobility

Geographical immobility occurs when workers are reluctant to move to a new region to take up work, which can result in available jobs and available workers not being located in the same area. There are a number of possible causes of this:

- *Regional house price differentials* — the cost of living varies dramatically between regions, making it difficult for home owners to relocate to more expensive areas such as the southeast of England.
- *Social and family ties* — individuals are unwilling to move away from their friends or relatives and do not want to disrupt their children's education by changing the school they attend.
- *Information failure* — it may be more difficult to find out about job availability in other areas. While the internet is reducing this information failure there is still a degree of local knowledge that is important in the job search process.

Occupational immobility

Occupational immobility occurs when workers are unable to transfer between occupations. This is a major cause of structural unemployment in the UK, as workers who have been made unemployed in the manufacturing sector have been unable to transition to employment in the service sector, for instance. The primary cause of occupational immobility is a lack of transferable skills. While firms could train workers to acquire these skills, firms are unwilling to make such an investment because of the threat of the trained workers being poached in the future. The result is that individuals who do not have the skills required for the occupations in which labour is being demanded find it difficult to gain employment.

Unemployment

There are a number of different types of unemployment that are of interest to labour market economists:

- *Frictional unemployment* — it is inevitable that some unemployment will exist as a result of individuals transitioning between jobs. Indeed, a degree of frictional unemployment is necessary for the labour market to be flexible. However, government policy to improve the ease of job search can help reduce the level of frictional unemployment.
- *Structural unemployment* — unemployment caused by skills mismatch (where those seeking work lack the skills required by employers) indicates a degree of inflexibility in the economy. While training can help overcome this problem, firms are reluctant to invest in high levels of training because they fear newly trained workers will be poached.
- *Voluntary unemployment* — unemployment can arise when individuals choose not to work because they assess themselves to be better off on benefits than accepting a low-paid job. This is most likely to occur when the **replacement ratio** is high and can lead to an unemployment trap, where workers choose to remain unemployed because they have no incentive to undertake work.

> **Knowledge check 18**
>
> Why might the labour force be more geographically immobile in the UK than in many other European countries?

> **Replacement ratio** The ratio of unemployment benefits to the wage that a claimant could receive in employment.

■ *Disequilibrium unemployment* — if the wage rate is set at a level above the market clearing wage rate, disequilibrium unemployment can occur. An example of this can be seen in Figure 27, where the wage rate is set at W_1 and there is disequilibrium unemployment equal to $(S_1 - D_1)$. Clearly, if wages were to adjust downwards, the labour market would equilibrate and there would be no disequilibrium unemployment. There are a number of reasons why wages might be unable to adjust. The existence of a minimum wage could prevent wages falling, while a wage rate of W_1 may have been achieved as a result of trade union negotiations. In fact, all employers, regardless of the presence of government or union intervention, find it difficult to cut nominal wages (wages are 'sticky' downwards as workers will not accept cuts to their nominal wages). This means that when demand for labour falls, disequilibrium unemployment is likely to be created, as firms are unable to reduce the wages as needed to reach the new equilibrium.

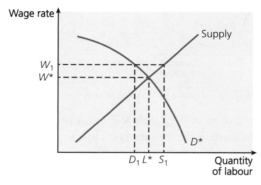

Figure 27 Disequilibrium unemployment

Informal labour markets

The informal labour market consists of individuals engaged in economic activity that is not registered or recorded. Such individuals are generating income without being formally employed or self-employed, which enables them to avoid paying tax and in doing so boost their real incomes. Firms are incentivised to employ individuals on an informal basis because it means they can avoid costly regulation associated with employing workers, such as paying national insurance contributions and paid holiday entitlement. Some markets operate in the informal sector because the activities themselves are illegal — drug dealing is a good example of this. While the informal economy is relatively small in the UK in comparison with other advanced nations, it is still estimated to account for approximately 10–13% of GDP.

Developing countries tend to have particularly large informal sectors. While some of this can be accounted for by subsistence agriculture, it often spreads into the wider economy. For example, as recently as 2010, more than 80% of India's non-agricultural employment was estimated to be in the informal sector. This creates a number of challenges for governments of developing countries. On the one hand, they want to reduce the size of the informal sector, as this will improve workers' employment protection as well as enabling much-needed tax revenue to be raised. On the other hand, however, they are wary of intervening and stifling entrepreneurship, which could worsen citizens' standard of living.

Knowledge check 19

Why is informal activity likely to be dominated by the service sector?

Government intervention on wages

Minimum wage

Introduced in 1999, the National Minimum Wage represents an hourly wage threshold below which it is illegal to employ workers. In 2015 it was set at £6.70 per hour for those aged over 21 and £5.30 for those aged 18–20. The impact of introducing a minimum wage in a perfectly competitive labour market is illustrated in Figure 28.

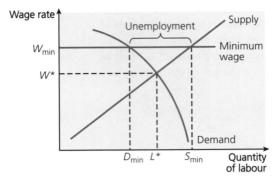

Figure 28 Implementing a minimum wage in a perfectly competitive labour market

Because firms are unable to employ workers below a wage of W_{min}, this will result in the wage rate increasing from W^* to W_{min}. This increase in firms' wage costs leads to a contraction along the demand curve for labour, causing the quantity of labour employed to fall from L^* to D_{min}. There are a number of arguments surrounding the effectiveness of a minimum wage, which can be summarised as in Table 3.

Table 3

Advantages	Disadvantages
Improves incentives to work by reducing the wage replacement ratio, therefore alleviating the poverty trap by reducing voluntary unemployment.	It creates unemployment of $(S_{min} - D_{min})$, possibly causing some individuals to transition from relative to absolute poverty by moving from a low wage to no wage. It also harms those who are already without work, who now find it even harder to get a job and may experience hysteresis as a consequence.
It reduces poverty by raising the income of the lowest earners, increasing their material standard of living and improving the distribution of income.	Many minimum-wage earners are not in poverty but are second-income earners in the household — the minimum wage is most commonly paid to individuals such as primary child-carers and students.

There is one special situation in which imposing a minimum wage can have an unambiguously positive impact — in the case of a monopsony employer. As shown in Figure 29, before the introduction of a minimum wage the monopsonist used its market power to set wages below the competitive equilibrium at W_0. If the government imposed a minimum wage at the competitive equilibrium, firms would no longer be able to exploit workers and would be forced to pay the competitive

Hysteresis
Unemployment causing long-term unemployment.

Exam tip

Unless told otherwise, when a question asks you to assess the impact of a minimum wage you should always start by assuming it is being imposed in a competitive labour market; you can then question this in evaluation.

equilibrium wage rate of W_{min}. Furthermore, no unemployment would be generated; in fact, the quantity of labour employed would actually increase from L_0 to L_{min}. This is because firms would no longer have the option to pay low wages by restricting the number of workers employed and so would choose to employ more workers — the marginal cost of hiring labour has effectively fallen as up to L_{min} firms are forced to pay the going-wage rate (the minimum wage) and so are not wage makers.

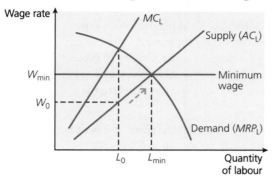

Figure 29 Minimum wage in the monopsony case

Living wage

The Living Wage Campaign argues that the National Minimum Wage is not providing sufficient income for individuals to live on. It has therefore used the Centre for Research in Social Policy at Loughborough University to estimate the wage an individual needs to afford an acceptable standard of living. There is recognition that the cost of living is significantly higher in London and this is reflected in a separate London living wage (which in 2015 stood at £9.15 an hour in comparison with the nationwide living wage of £7.85). While firms are not legally required to pay the living wage to their workers, many have chosen to do so in the face of public pressure in order to maintain a good reputation with consumers.

Maximum wage

The 2008 financial crisis put increased focus on the very high wages earned by investment bankers, with some commentators arguing a maximum wage should be imposed to improve equity in the labour market and narrow the distribution of income. While this could clearly cause great harm to incentives, there is some debate as to the extent to which this represents a realistic concern; the relatively small substitution effect present for high earners demonstrates that incentive effects are not particularly significant at high levels of income. The government has resisted implementing maximum wages to date as such a policy could result in human capital flight. In a globalised world in which the highest paid are often the most skilled and therefore the most geographically mobile, there is a desire to retain high earners by implementing modest, if any, tax increases.

Government intervention

There are a number of policies available to the government to reduce the labour market failure that occurs, many of which are detailed over the subsequent pages.

Knowledge check 20

What would be the impact of varying the minimum wage by region?
·······························

Legislation and regulation

There are a number of laws in place related to health and safety in the workplace. Without such laws labour market failure would exist — firms would aim to keep costs as low as possible in order to maximise profit and therefore show little regard for workers' safety, while workers would perhaps suffer from information failure in not recognising the benefits of taking appropriate care of themselves at work.

The most significant piece of legislation in place is the EU Working Time Directive, designed to limit working hours and set minimum conditions for annual leave entitlement. The UK government has implemented a range of other policies to protect workers' safety in specific industries, particularly in professions such as construction where firms are required to train workers to pass specific qualifications before they are allowed to employ them.

While this could overcome the labour market failure previously described, it has the potential to generate a new form of labour market failure, as shown in Figure 30. Complying with legislation adds cost to employing workers, causing the average cost of labour to be above the supply of labour. Because firms will employ workers where the average cost of labour (equivalent to the marginal cost of labour in a perfectly competitive labour market) is equal to the marginal revenue product of labour, this means employment will fall below the competitive equilibrium to L_1. Firms will pay workers on the labour supply curve at W_1. The result is that while workers may benefit from improved protection, this comes at the cost of lower wages.

Exam tip

Laws set on a European level such as the Working Time Directive are not always fully adopted by the UK. The UK was late to adopt this directive and workers currently have the choice to opt out of following the directive, with many choosing to work beyond the prescribed limit of 48 hours a week.

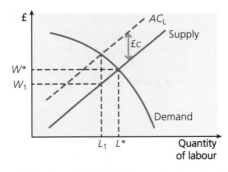

Figure 30 The impact of health and safety legislation

Education and training

A lack of education and training is a significant cause of labour market failure. Individuals do not undertake sufficient education because of information failure and employers do not train workers to the optimal level because they fear such workers will be poached by rival firms. This results in occupational immobility and causes structural unemployment, as individuals seeking work lack the skills required in order to take up employment.

There is a range of policy measures in place designed to tackle this market failure. The government offers a selection of employability training to the unemployed, attendance at which is compulsory in order to be eligible to receive unemployment benefits. A range of subsidies is also on offer to firms that offer training or employment to the unemployed. Such investment is heavily focused on younger age groups, with an increasing number of apprenticeship programmes available to give young people the chance to gain the experience required to participate in the labour market. The combination of these measures should improve labour market flexibility and productivity.

Trade union reform

To avoid the higher wages, lower levels of employment and disruption of strike action that trade unions can cause, the government can seek to limit their influence by implementing anti-union legislation. The most significant period of this occurred in the 1980s, when the Thatcher government introduced laws such as the requirement for union members to be balloted before a strike could be undertaken. This limited unions' ability to surprise firms with short-notice strikes, thus reducing the potential disruption that strikes could cause by giving firms a warning period while the ballot was being conducted and enabling them to put in place alternative arrangements. Reducing the power of trade unions in this way has contributed to the decline in union membership since the legislation was introduced.

Knowledge check 21

How have changes in the structure of economic activity affected trade union membership?

Regional policy

Geographical immobility causes a number of problems in the labour market, including wage differentials between areas and high unemployment in some regions. Regional policy is designed to overcome these problems and tends to involve incentives being given to either individuals or firms. Regional house price differentials and the large deposits required to purchase properties in high-employment areas are major barriers to many individuals; the government can help reduce this by offering cheaper mortgage deals or contributions towards a deposit to enable the labour market to clear — the 'Help to Buy' scheme operating in 2015 is good example of this, with the government supporting mortgages that allow individuals to purchase a house with only a 5% deposit.

However, given that family ties mean many individuals will not relocate even if they are offered financial support to do so, the government has increasingly focused on incentivising firms to relocate to regions of high unemployment. They can do this by offering grants and tax breaks as financial incentives or investing in infrastructure to attract firms to an area by creating enterprise zones. The government can take the lead in encouraging firms to relocate by moving public sector organisations. In recent years many civil service functions have been moved outside of London — for instance, a large volume of BBC output is now produced from Salford in the northwest of England.

Reforming the tax and benefits system

To reduce voluntary unemployment and improve incentives to work, the government can reform the tax and benefits system to make work pay. One example of this is raising the personal income tax allowance. By 2015 the income individuals can earn before paying any income tax had risen from £6,475 in 2010 to £10,600. This incentivises individuals to enter the labour market as they are now able to keep a larger proportion of their income. Thus the wage-replacement ratio is reduced and therefore the opportunity cost of remaining unemployed increases. This can help to reduce reliance on benefits.

Exam tip

Raising the personal allowance is an example of a policy designed to make the tax system more progressive.

Tax cuts of this sort are expensive, however. One way to fund this is by reducing welfare benefits, which can have the added advantage of incentivising individuals into the labour market by reducing the wage-replacement ratio. There is debate among economists concerning the fairness of such a strategy, with some arguing it pushes those who are genuinely unable to find or participate in employment into absolute poverty.

Pensions and immigration

The ageing population resulting from rising life expectancy and a falling birth rate is contributing to what is sometimes referred to as a demographic time-bomb, with increasing state pension and healthcare expenditure putting significant pressure on the government budget. One solution to this is to raise the retirement age. This is being implemented gradually from the current age of 65 so that by 2046 it will be 68. While this policy will reduce government spending and increase the productive capacity of the economy, it is politically unpopular and takes a long time to have an impact on government finances.

The government has also tried to increase the take-up of private pensions through the introduction of auto-enrolment, whereby all employees are automatically enrolled in their workplace pension scheme and now have to opt out if they do not want to participate. The aim of this policy is to reduce retired individuals' dependence on the state. In the UK the potential crisis caused by an ageing population has been partially offset by high levels of immigration. An influx of skilled workers has helped boost the productive capacity of the economy, increased tax revenue and enabled the government to cope with rising public spending demands. Clearly, though, immigration also brings with it its own challenges, including having to develop infrastructure to cope with an expanding population.

Knowledge check 22

Why could private pensions be described as a merit good?

Summary

After studying the topic of the *Labour market* you should be able to:

- Explain the concept of derived demand and the factors determining the demand (marginal revenue product) and elasticity of demand for labour in an industry.
- Explain the factors determining the supply and elasticity of supply of labour in an industry.
- Evaluate, using a diagram, how the substitution and income effects determine an individual's labour supply in the short run.
- Understand and illustrate diagrammatically the difference between transfer earnings and economic rent.
- Explain what is meant by unit labour costs and evaluate the implications of international variations in unit labour costs.

- Evaluate, using diagrams, how wages are determined in competitive labour markets and why wage differentials exist.
- Evaluate the impact of a monopsonist employer on the labour market.
- Understand the trends in trade union membership and evaluate diagrammatically the impact they have on a competitive and monopsonist labour market.
- Evaluate, using diagrams, the impact of maximum, minimum and living wages on the labour market.
- Evaluate the causes and consequences of immobility and inflexibility of labour.
- Evaluate the impact of discrimination, migration and demographic changes on the labour market.
- Evaluate the significance of informal labour markets.
- Evaluate the various policies available to the government to correct labour market failure.

■ Market failure and government intervention

Environment

Functions of the environment

The environment fulfils three crucial functions in the economy:

■ *Provider of resources* — firms need a variety of natural resources, such as oil and gas, in the production process.

■ *Provider of amenities* — individuals derive utility (happiness) from the amenities the environment provides, such as enjoying walking in the countryside or relaxing on a beach.

■ *Absorber of waste* — firms and households generate waste, which needs to be absorbed by the environment.

It is questionable whether the environment can continue to provide these three functions indefinitely, as there are clear trade-offs between them. For example, continuing to use the environment as an absorber of waste may damage its ability to provide resources and amenities in the future. In order for development to be sustainable, economic growth must meet the needs of the present without compromising the ability of future generations to meet their own needs. Any growth that results in environmental degradation, then, would not be considered sustainable, as future generations would be inheriting a stock of resources that is insufficient to enable them to have the same quality of life as the generation before them.

Externalities

The production process in many industries causes environmental harm. When a computer manufacturer is choosing how many computers to produce, it is considering its own costs and benefits of production, producing an output at Q_1, as illustrated in Figure 31. The market fails because the producer is failing to take into account the pollution the production demonstrates and the subsequent harm this does to the atmosphere. This means marginal social cost exceeds marginal private cost and there is over-production of $(Q_1 - Q^*)$. The welfare loss generated in the negative externalities of production case is illustrated by the shaded region in the figure.

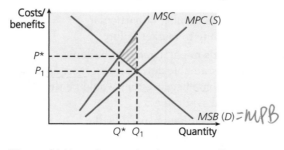

Figure 31 Negative production externality

Knowledge check 23

Why is the optimal level of pollution not zero?

Consumption can also cause negative externalities. For example, when one individual chooses to use a beach they are considering their own private benefits, which come from relaxing in the sunshine; they are not considering the potential harms they are causing to other beach users, who enjoy the beach less because it is overcrowded. If individuals considered the harms they were causing to third parties when using the beach, fewer individuals would go to the beach. This is illustrated in Figure 32, with over-consumption of the beach represented by $(Q_2 - Q^*)$.

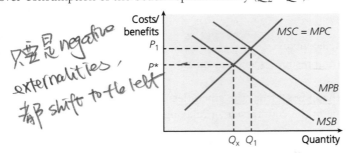

Figure 32 Negative consumption externality

Finally, there are also cases in which there are positive environmental externalities associated with the production or consumption of a good. An example of this is the use of public transport such as bus travel in London. While some individuals will choose to ride the bus because it gives them increased leisure time (they can read or sleep while on the bus, which they couldn't do when driving), there will generally be under-consumption if left to the free market, as individuals will ignore the environmental benefits that come from travelling by bus in terms of reduced pollution. There will therefore be a welfare loss of the shaded region, as illustrated in Figure 33.

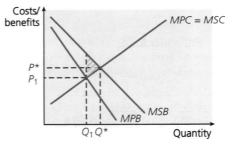

Figure 33 Positive consumption externality

In addition to traditional externalities theory, there are a number of particular problems associated with the environment that contribute to market failure:

■ *NIMBY syndrome* — while the majority of individuals might agree that building nuclear power stations would contribute towards sustainable development, most are unlikely to agree to having one built close to their home because they would be the ones to suffer. This is known as 'not in my back yard syndrome'.

■ *International disagreement* — the damage to the environment caused by the emission of greenhouse gases leads to global problems and requires global consensus to achieve a meaningful solution. The problem is that countries do not agree on the best way to tackle climate change and therefore struggle to reach agreement, as has been illustrated by the problems associated with enforcing the Kyoto Accord.

Environmental Kuznets curve

The environmental Kuznets curve charts the relationship between economic growth and environmental degradation. This is illustrated in Figure 34, with pollution initially increasing as the economy grows before decreasing as per capita income continues to rise above y^*.

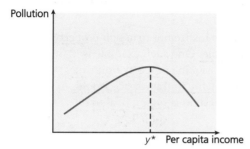

Figure 34 Environmental Kuznets curve

Exam tip

In many developing countries manufacturing accounts for a significantly higher proportion of GDP than in developed countries, which offers a further explanation for why economic growth is likely to harm the environment in developing economies.

The fact that developing economies often see environmental harm increasing as they experience economic growth can be explained by a number of factors:

- Industries are growing but are likely to be reliant on inefficient and polluting technology.
- As incomes rise, the demand for cars and other goods and services that make demands on the environment, such as electricity, is likely to be increasing rapidly.

The situation is different for developed economies where per capita income already exceeds y^*. As these countries experience economic growth, pollution is likely to fall because:

- businesses may be able to adopt cleaner and more efficient production technology
- the growth in demand for car ownership will fall because most individuals will already own cars
- the government may be able to devote more resources to protecting the environment as there is less pressure to alleviate poverty (as absolute poverty is very low in developed economies).

The impact of economic growth on the environment clearly depends upon whether the growth has been delivered using renewable resources. In a sense the market mechanism will work to ensure growth is not unsustainable — rising oil prices in recent years caused by the depletion of the stock of this resource have resulted in firms investing in alternatives to oil, such as electric cars. However, the rate of economic growth in some countries, such as India and China, has arguably increased the rate at which resources are depleted; if renewable sources of energy cannot be developed quickly enough to meet rising demand then such growth is clearly unsustainable and will generate environmental harms.

[handwritten: Environmental depletion]

The tragedy of the commons *[handwritten: Over-produced. (negative externalities of production)]*

The tragedy of the commons occurs because of a lack of property rights. A good example of this is fishing. Because no one owns the sea there is likely to be over-fishing — each fisherman is motivated solely by the income they can gain from catching fish and does not take into account the harm they will be causing to fishermen in the future by depleting the stock of fish. Essentially, the problem comes because the sea is a quasi-public good — catching fish is rivalrous but non-excludable. Clearly, if one individual, organisation or country owned the sea it would be in their interests to ensure over-fishing would not take place, as it would decrease the value of their asset.

Therefore, the solution to the tragedy of the commons is to attempt to assign property rights. However, this is not always practical or enforceable. One such example is in the case of noise pollution caused by aircraft — while assigning property rights of the sky to local residents who could charge airlines for flying in their space would internalise the negative externality, realistically such a system is impractical to implement and coordinate. *[handwritten: 不切实际、]*

[handwritten: 实施]

Environmental policy

Taxation

Figure 35 illustrates the impact of imposing a pollution tax on a firm whose production generates negative externalities.

[handwritten left margin: Too high
→ Inequality ↑
→ black market
* ↳ less tax revenue*
* ↳ not safe to use.*
→ Inelastic PED
* (very high tax needed to reduce demand)*
→ Inflation
→ Tax here greater impact on less wealthy people (progressive) tobacco]

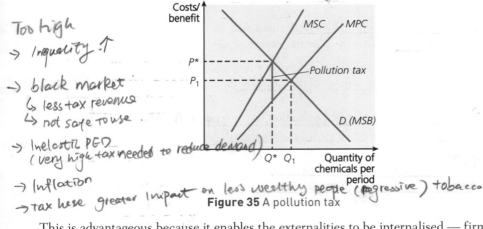

Figure 35 A pollution tax

This is advantageous because it enables the externalities to be internalised — firms are made to pay for the harms they are causing to third parties, making marginal private cost equal to marginal social cost and resulting in output falling to Q^*. However, this is effective only if the government can correctly identify the size of the external cost, which in practice is very difficult. This means the tax is unlikely to be set at the right level, meaning the tax may either be too small to fully correct the market failure or too large and therefore cause government failure.

There is debate among economists as to whether tax revenue raised should be hypothecated. The principle of tax hypothecation is that revenues raised from a particular tax should be dedicated to a particular purpose. For example, some motorists argue it is unfair that the taxes raised from petrol are not all used to improve

[handwritten: taxing transport]

> **Exam tip**
>
> The London congestion charge is an example of hypothecation — all revenue raised by the scheme is used to fund improvements in London's transport infrastructure.

road infrastructure. While hypothecation seems to make it easier to justify imposing a tax, in reality it puts unnecessary restrictions on the government, which may want to use the revenue for a range of purposes, including to directly or indirectly compensate any third parties that have been harmed in the production process.

Regulation

Another option available to the government is to impose laws or restrictions, such as putting a limit on firms' emissions levels. This is desirable because it enables a specific level of pollution to be achieved and is a more direct method of solving the market failure than imposing a tax, which treats all firms indiscriminately according to the size of their output rather than the level of their pollution. However, this again creates issues of whether the government has sufficient knowledge to determine the optimal level of pollution, and also presents problems in terms of enforcement — constantly monitoring things such as an individual firm's level of pollution is both difficult and expensive. *administration*

— Correct level:
Too small — problems cannot be solved.
Too high — firms try to avoid being detected

— we do not always know who the polluter is.

— Enforcement
difficult and expensive to monitoring

— black market
illegal supplies through black market may result

Subsidising public transport

Subsidising public transport can help reduce pollution by encouraging individuals to switch away from travelling by car. Figure 36 illustrates the impact of subsidising a train company.

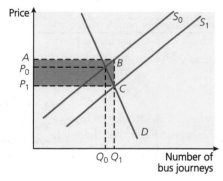

Figure 36 A public transport subsidy

Subsidies =
① cost
(补贴越是 Price Inelastic demand)
② set the right level (Perfect information?)
under subsidise (not solve MF)
over subsidise — inefficient firms
③ firms do not use money to increase output.
(more dividends to to shareholders)
(save in banks)
(high wages)
④ Price Inelastic demand

By reducing the price of travelling by train there should be an extension along the demand curve and a subsequent increase in the number of individuals travelling by train. This should reduce the number travelling by car, thus reducing congestion and pollution. However, this clearly depends upon the elasticity of demand. Given that demand is likely to be price inelastic for train travel (demand may not be that sensitive to changes in price, as most individuals have a preferred mode of transport and trains often do not stop at the destinations individuals want to go from or to), the subsidy would need to be very large to have a significant enough impact on train usage. If combined with other policies to deter car use, though, such as increasing road tax, it is likely to have a positive impact.

Knowledge check 24

Identify the size of the train subsidy illustrated in Figure 36.

⑤ opportunity cost of money spent on subsidy.

Tradable pollution permits

To solve the negative externalities caused by pollution the government could implement a tradable pollution permits system, where firms have to own permits in order to be able to pollute, with each permit allowing a firm to emit a certain amount of pollution. Firms are able to buy and sell permits from each other, creating a market for permits. There are a number of arguments for and against such a system:

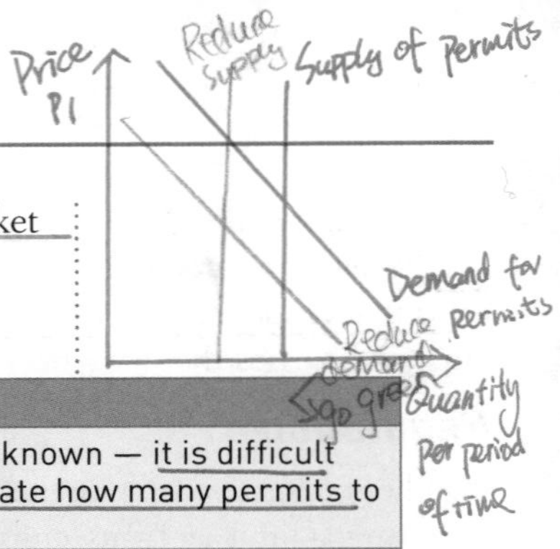

Table 4 *[handwritten: global cooperation]*

Advantages	Disadvantages
Enables a specific level of pollution to be achieved — total pollution in the market will be limited by the total number of permits.	Optimal level of pollution unknown — it is difficult for the government to estimate how many permits to allocate.
Polluter pays principle holds — those firms causing the most harms to third parties (i.e. polluting the most) will require the most permits and therefore experience the highest cost. A firm that is large but relatively clean in its production methods will not be harmed in the way it would be from a tax on output.	Allocation issues — the government will find it difficult to decide how to fairly allocate permits. This could be done via an auction, but this has the potential to reduce competitiveness if one or two big firms buy up all the permits. The permits could be grandfathered — given to the largest firms — but this would increase barriers to entry.
Provides an incentive for firms to go green — if firms clean up their production they can sell their permits to other firms.	Difficult to enforce — firms may pollute beyond the number of permits they have and this will be difficult and costly to police.

Information *[handwritten: not fully understand the failure.]*

In some instances environmental harm could simply be caused by a lack of information. This could potentially be fixed by investing in information campaigns and improving education on particular issues, such as encouraging people to recycle. However, the issue with such campaigns is that individuals do not care about harms to third parties; they may know that recycling would be good for the environment, but they simply ignore this when making decisions. *[handwritten: People just ignore the information]*

Public–private partnerships *[handwritten: 私人融资活动]*

In 1992, the Private Finance Initiative (PFI) was launched in an attempt to involve the private sector in the provision of public services. The principle is that the public sector invites private firms to submit bids to carry out a particular piece of work, such as constructing a new toll road. Such work can be done either exclusively by the private firm or in partnership with the public sector. The private firm then gets a return from such investment either from direct payment by the government or from being entitled to revenue generated by the project — in this example, the toll road revenue. *[handwritten: Public good do not need to be provided by the government but private sector involvement may be encouraged.]*

The attraction of such a policy is that it introduces competition into the public sector, which should improve efficiency. It also reduces the pressure on public financing of big infrastructure projects, thereby enabling a greater number of projects to be carried out. However, there are some criticisms of this. Given that private firms are motivated by profit, it is likely to mean the cost of the service is higher than it would be if provided by the public sector, while a private firm is likely to experience higher borrowing costs than the government would. Finally, some argue that private firms may be more likely to cut corners, putting users' safety at risk, in order to maximise profit in the way that the public sector would not.

Exam tip

It is important to understand the significant scale of the PFI – by 2012 it had contributed to the completion of more than 700 projects, representing more than £55 billion of private sector investment in the public sector.

[handwritten margin note top right: Price P1 / Reduce supply Supply of permits / Demand for permits / Reduce demand / Sap, greQuantity per period of time]

Alternative methods of government intervention

Competition policy

The Competition and Markets Authority (CMA) is responsible for investigating anti-competitive practices in markets to ensure firms do not abuse their market power. Having defined the relevant market by deciding which products should be included within the market, the CMA will investigate any mergers or acquisitions that result in a firm having a UK market share of more than 25%.

In 2007 the Competition Commission (the pre-cursor to the CMA) investigated the British Airports Authority (BAA), which at the time owned London airports Heathrow, Gatwick and Stansted, and Scottish airports Edinburgh, Glasgow and Aberdeen. The company had a 90% share of the air travel market in the southeast of England and an 84% market share in Scotland. The investigation found that BAA's market power reduced the incentives to expand and improve the quality of provision that would be present in a more competitive market. The Competition Commission therefore instructed BAA to sell off some of its airports to increase the level of competition in the market — by 2015 it had sold Gatwick, Stansted and Edinburgh airports.

Cost–benefit analysis

The basic economic problem dictates that the government has to make choices over how to allocate its scarce resources. One method for doing this is by using social cost–benefit analysis, which essentially brings together both the direct and indirect costs and benefits of a particular project in order to determine whether it is viable. There are several stages involved in such analysis:

1. *Identify relevant costs and benefits* — the direct costs are relatively easy to identify, such as the production costs of building a new school and the labour costs of employing more teachers. The indirect/external costs are less straightforward and require consideration of the concept of opportunity cost — how could the land that the school is being built on have been used and are there negative impacts on local residents of a school being built close by? Finally, direct benefits (improved income in the future for the individuals that become more educated) and indirect benefits (greater productivity leading to higher tax revenue) need to be identified.

2. *Valuation* — the costs and benefits then need to be assigned monetary values in order for them to be compared. Many of them, such as the cost of construction materials, have a price attached to them, making them easy to value. However, for indirect costs and benefits such as externalities, a shadow price needs to be assigned, which estimates the monetary value of each item. This is clearly a subjective process.

3. *Discounting the future* — costs or benefits that occur in the future need to be expressed in terms of their value in the present. Future costs and benefits therefore need to be 'discounted', as a benefit that occurs immediately is clearly more valuable than a benefit of the same amount

A Government may choose different discount rates depending on wether it wants to benefit future generations or current one.

that occurs only 50 years from now. A <u>discount rate</u> therefore has to be applied to <u>calculate the net present value of costs and benefits</u>. Clearly the <u>size of the discount rate</u> depends upon a judgement over the relative importance of the short and long term. The government is likely to set a lower discount rate than consumers, as unlike consumers, who are primarily motivated by the here and now, the government will be partly concerned with the impact on future generations.

Once this process has been conducted, the total net benefits can be divided by the total net costs to produce a benefit:cost ratio. While social-cost benefit analysis is flawed because of the number of assumptions required in conducting the steps outlined above, its strength is that it allows for relatively accurate comparisons to be made between projects when the same assumptions are used throughout. For example, if the benefit:cost ratio is calculated to be 2.4 for building a new school compared with 1.3 for building a new hospital, this provides strong evidence to the government that its scarce resources should be allocated towards building the school rather than the hospital.

Knowledge check 25

Identify the costs and benefits involved in the government undertaking the Crossrail project in London, a £14.8 billion new train line connecting East and West London.

Summary

After studying the topic of _Market failure and government intervention_ you should be able to:
- Explain the functions of the environment.
- Explain, using diagrams, how production and consumption can generate environmental externalities.
- Explain, using a diagram, the environmental Kuznets curve and evaluate the extent to which economic growth contributes to environmental degradation.
- Evaluate the effectiveness of policies used to reduce the rate of environmental degradation.
- Explain how competition policy can be used to correct market failure in product markets.
- Understand what is meant by cost–benefit analysis and evaluate its value in helping governments to make decisions.

4. Calculate the difference between costs and benefits — the net present value.

If the ∧net present value is positive → worthwhile.

而我们要计算的 是：

① Present value benefit (PVB)
Present value cost (PVC)
PVB − PVC = net present value (NPV)
If NPV positive = overall net benefit.

② Benefit to cost ratio.
PV benefits : PV costs
↑
high = better.

Questions & Answers

This section provides an explanation of the structure of the A-level Component 1: Microeconomics and Component 3: Themes in Economics exams, together with strategies for approaching the different types of questions you will encounter. This is followed by a series of sample questions covering all the question types — multiple-choice, data-response and essays. After all of these questions there are some example answers from students. You should practise all of these questions yourself and compare your answers to these while reading the detailed comments on the answers to improve your understanding of what is required to achieve full marks.

Assessment objectives

To succeed in this course you will need to be able to demonstrate your ability in the following assessment objectives:

AO	Key skill	Explanation	Weighting at A-level
1	Knowledge	Demonstrate knowledge of terms/concepts and theories/models.	22.5%
2	Application	Apply knowledge and understanding to various economic contexts.	25%
3	Analysis	Analyse issues within economics, showing an understanding of their impact on economic agents.	25%
4	Evaluation	Evaluate economic arguments and use qualitative and quantitative evidence to support informed judgements relating to economic issues.	27.5%

■ Component 1: Microeconomics

This is examined by a 120-minute paper. There are 80 marks awarded for the paper; you therefore have approximately 90 seconds to answer each question.

The content covered in the paper will include everything in this book alongside the Year 1 Microeconomics content covered in *Student Guide 1*.

The paper is split into three sections:

- **Section A — Data-response**
  - You will be given a variety of stimulus material, which is most likely to focus on a particular market. You will then be asked a series of questions related to this market, which tests the full range of assessment objectives. Questions will range in value from straightforward 2 mark questions to an 8 and a 12 mark question, both of which are level marked in the same way as the essays.
  - The section is worth a total of 30 marks and you should aim to spend approximately 40 minutes on it.

- **Section B — Quantitative essay questions**
  - You will be given a choice of two essay questions and must answer one of these. The answer will require you to demonstrate some quantitative skills, most likely through drawing a diagram.
  - The essay is worth 25 marks and you should aim to spend approximately 40 minutes on it.
- **Section C — Qualitative essay questions**
  - You will be given a choice of two essay questions and must answer one of these. These essays will not require you to demonstrate any quantitative skills but you may well find a diagram will support your discussion; relevant diagrams will be credited.
  - The essay is worth 25 marks and you should aim to spend approximately 40 minutes on it.

■ Component 3: Themes in Economics

This is examined by a 120-minute paper. There are 80 marks awarded for the paper; you therefore have approximately 90 seconds to answer each question.

The content covered in the paper will include everything in the A-level Economics specification, summarised by all four *Student Guides*.

The paper is split into two sections:
- **Section A — Multiple choice**
  - You will be asked 30 multiple-choice questions covering the whole A-level Economics specification. These could require you to conduct simple calculations, interpret points on diagrams or recall knowledge about technical theory.
  - Each question is worth 1 mark and you will have to select the correct answer from a choice of four options.
  - You should aim to spend approximately 45 minutes on this section.
- **Section B — Data-response**
  - You will be given a variety of stimulus material focusing on a particular theme. You will then be asked a series of questions related to this theme, which tests the full range of assessment objectives and requires use of both micro- and macroeconomic theory. Questions will range in value from straightforward 2 mark questions to level-marked 15 mark questions.
  - The section is worth a total of 50 marks and you should aim to spend approximately 75 minutes on it.

When answering multiple-choice questions you should do the following:
- Work through them quickly — remember, you have only 90 seconds on average to complete each one. Some will take longer than this, but that should be compensated by others that are much quicker to complete. Do not spend too long on any one question.
- Cover up the options when reading the question and see whether you can work out the answer before looking at the four options — this is often quicker than reading the options and getting distracted by those that are incorrect but are close to being right.

- If unsure, eliminate those answers you know to be incorrect and choose between any options you have left — there is no penalty for answering incorrectly so you should never leave an answer blank.
- When practising multiple-choice questions in the build-up to the exam, try to justify why the incorrect options are incorrect. This is done in the example multiple-choice questions in this guide.

When answering data-response questions you should:

- Read the stimulus material very carefully, remembering to refer to it in your answers when required.
- Work out which assessment objectives the question is testing — do not waste time evaluating when the question is only asking you to offer an explanation.
- Make sure you always fully apply your answer to the market in the question; avoid producing theoretical answers that ignore the specifics given in the case study.

Answering essay questions

The most important thing to remember when answering essay questions is to cover each of the four skills tested by the assessment objectives. These essays, along with any questions that require evaluation in the data-response section, are level marked. Which level your answer is placed in depends upon how well you have covered each of the four skills — these are graded as being 'Limited', 'Reasonable', 'Good' or 'Strong'. Aim to get into the strong category on all skills, as detailed in the table.

	AO1 and AO2	AO3	AO4
Limited	Awareness of the meaning of the terms in the question.	Simple statement(s) of cause and effect.	An unsupported assertion.
Reasonable	As above and applied to the context of the question.	An explanation of causes and consequences, which omits some key links in the chain of argument.	Some attempt to come to a conclusion, which shows some recognition of influencing factors.
Good	Precision in the use of the terms in the question and applied in a focused way to the context of the question.	An explanation of causes and consequences, developing most of the links in the chain of argument.	A conclusion is drawn weighing up both sides, but without reaching a supported judgement.
Strong		An explanation of causes and consequences, fully developing the links in the chain of argument.	A conclusion is drawn weighing up both sides, and reaches a supported judgement.

Generally, the best way to approach these questions is to fully analyse one side of the argument, analyse the other side and then reach a judgement saying which side of the argument is stronger and why you have reached this conclusion. This is likely to include a consideration of the factors your judgement depends upon.

A-level Microeconomics Section A

Data-response

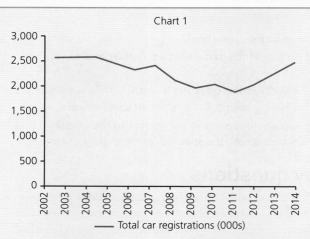

Chart 1

Total car registrations (000s)

Following a decline in demand as a result of the financial crisis, the sale of new cars has been rising steadily in recent years, caused largely by an increase in the number of multi-car households. By far the most popular car manufacturer in the UK is Ford, with a market share of 13.25% in 2014, largely driven by the success of its popular Fiesta model. It is facing increasing competition around the world, however, including in China where in 2015 it significantly cut its prices in response to Volkswagen AG discounting several popular vehicles. Competition in the UK market is also increasing, with Ford seeing its market share decline slowly year on year (in 2013 it stood at 13.8%).

While increased competition has generally been considered good for consumers, who have experienced falling prices, there are concerns that increasing car usage is contributing to long-term environmental damage, such as pollution and global warming. As car ownership has continued to rise, one solution to the environmental harms it causes has emerged in the form of the growth of the alternatively fuelled vehicles (AFVs) market. In March 2015 more than 6,000 plug-in cars were purchased — a 400% increase on sales a year earlier.

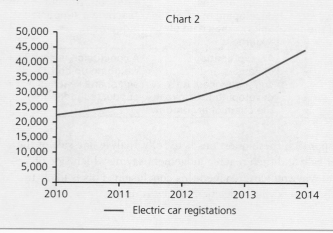

Chart 2

Electric car registations

There are a number of factors contributing to the growth in this market, including increased choice for the consumer — the number of plug-in vehicle models available has risen from just 6 in 2011 to 27 in 2015. A government grant that offers up to £5,000 off the cost of electric vehicles has further incentivised consumers to switch away from traditional petrol- or diesel-based vehicles. To date the government has already invested in excess of £500 million in the electric vehicles market, including providing grants to firms to construct charging points around the country.

Many of the largest firms are making significant profits. Volkswagen leads the way, reporting an annual profit of approximately £18 billion in 2014, with Ford's profit in the region of £14 billion. Nissan, which is currently spending huge amounts on developing its electric 'Leaf' model, has a more modest profit level of £2.2 billion. One of the more surprising profit figures comes from Peugeot, which, despite being one of the largest manufacturers, recorded just a £0.5 billion profit. This led to the company focusing on cost-cutting methods in an attempt to improve profitability. Chery International, a state-owned Chinese car producer, has not implemented such cost-cutting measures, despite making more cars than it sells for several years.

(a) Using Charts 1 and 2, explain the trends in the purchase of new cars between 2010 and 2014. (2 marks)

ℯ Identify the key trends present in Charts 1 and 2 and note any similarities or differences you observe.

(b) Explain, using a diagram, the market failure that arises from car use. (4 marks)

ℯ First decide whether the question is referring to consumption or production externalities here and then decide whether such externalities are positive or negative. Draw the appropriate diagram and refer to it when explaining the market failure that occurs.

(c) Explain whether there is any evidence of firms in the car industry engaging in predatory pricing. (4 marks)

ℯ Explain what is meant by predatory pricing and look for evidence in the case study to either support or disagree with the suggestion that car manufacturers are engaged in predatory pricing.

(d) The government is continuing to provide grants of up to £5,000 to individuals who purchase electric vehicles, but has recently ended grants offered to firms constructing electric vehicle charging points.
Evaluate the role of social cost–benefit analysis in making decisions such as this. (8 marks)

ℯ The directive word 'evaluate' means a two-sided answer is required here. Explain what social cost–benefit analysis is and apply it to the particular investment decisions being made in this question. Consider the limitations of social cost–benefit analysis before reaching a supported judgement.

(e) Using evidence from the stimulus material, evaluate the extent to which firms in the car industry are behaving as profit maximisers. (12 marks)

ℯ A two-sided answer is required here with a supported judgement. You should use the stimulus material throughout to provide evidence of profit-maximising behaviour in the car industry. You should also consider other possible objectives car manufacturers may be pursuing before reaching a supported judgement.

Student A

(a) Overall, the number of new car registrations has increased every year since 2010. This is also true of electric car registrations. The growth rate in the purchase of such vehicles is significantly higher than the overall growth rate — while the purchase of new cars overall increased by approximately 22%, the purchase of electric vehicles more than doubled over the same time period.

ⓔ **2/2 marks awarded.** The upward trend in both charts is identified and the student recognises that the trend is stronger for electric cars. There is effective use of the data to provide supporting evidence, having correctly calculated the percentage increase in the number of new cars registered over the 4-year period.

(b) When driving cars consumers do not consider the harms they are causing to third parties as a result of their consumption. The consequence is that there is a divergence between marginal social benefit and marginal private benefit, causing overconsumption of (Q_1-Q^*), which results in a welfare loss — if consumers took into account the environmental harms they were causing, either fewer people would drive cars or they would drive them less often.

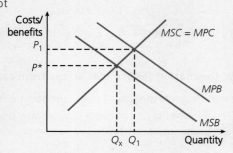

ⓔ **3/4 marks awarded.** A correct diagram supported by a strong technical explanation of the market failure that is taking place as a result of negative externalities of consumption. The answer would be better if specific examples of the environmental harms resulting from car use were provided.

(c) There is no evidence of firms engaging in predatory pricing. The extract refers to Volkswagen cutting prices and Ford cutting prices in response, which suggests there is price competition in the market. This does not suggest, though, any predatory pricing, i.e. a firm setting prices below costs in order to eliminate the competition. This is because even when Ford cut its prices it still saw its market share fall (from 13.8% to 13.25%) — this would not have happened if it had been predatory pricing, as it would have stolen the market share of rival firms it had forced out of business. Moreover, at the end of the extract there is reference to Volkswagen and Ford making substantial profits (£18 billion and £14 billion respectively). Such profits would not be present if predatory pricing was occurring.

ⓔ 4/4 marks awarded. The student shows an excellent understanding of the concept of predatory pricing, making a clear distinction between price competition and predatory pricing. Clear evidence is provided from the case study, both in terms of Ford's declining market share and high profit levels, to demonstrate that Ford cannot be engaged in predatory pricing.

(d) Social cost–benefit analysis (CBA) can be used by the government to make decisions over its expenditure. By identifying all social costs and benefits associated with the investment and assigning a monetary value to them, the costs and benefits can be weighed up against each other and a decision can be made as to whether it is a sensible investment. This is needed because there are at any one time more projects the government could fund than the government has tax revenue to spend, meaning choices need to be made over how to allocate scarce resources. Social cost–benefit analysis provides a scientific framework through which such decisions can be taken to ensure the government allocates its scarce resources where they are most needed.

However, the value of such analysis depends upon whether correct values can be assigned to the costs and benefits. While relatively straightforward to achieve with direct costs and benefits, this is much more difficult for external costs and benefits, which cannot easily be monetised. The more difficult it is to accurately estimate these shadow prices, the less likely it is that social cost–benefit analysis will deliver a robust result that can be relied upon. Moreover, the result of such analysis crucially depends upon the discount rate used. Many of the benefits to the environment from investment in electric vehicles will only be enjoyed in the long run, when future generations benefit from a less polluted atmosphere. Clearly, future benefits are not as valuable to individuals today as current benefits are, meaning such benefits need to be 'discounted' using a discount rate. The rate to use for this, though, is far from obvious — given the conclusions CBA reaches could alter when the discount rate is changed, this again means it is not an objective measure for the government to use when making decisions.

In conclusion, while there are some constraints involved in conducting CBA, providing the same assumptions are used to compare projects it does provide a sensible way for the government to reach decisions such as continuing to give grants for the purchase of electric vehicles and to end grants for the construction of charging terminals. It is even more valuable when the government is presented with a range of different estimates based on different assumptions; comparing these side by side will enable the government to reach a fully informed decision.

ⓔ 6/8 marks awarded. Strong analysis is offered here, with a clear exposition of how social cost–benefit analysis operates. The analysis could have been improved if greater attention was given to the specific example given in the question —

providing an illustration in the context of electric vehicles would have helped. The evaluation is superb, with impressive technical reference to the concept of shadow prices and an accurate explanation of the issues associated with estimating the discount rate. The answer reaches a clear supported judgement, which essentially recognises that, while not perfect, CBA can be informative and useful for the government.

(e) Entrepreneurs who own car manufacturers take risks in organising factors of production in order to make a profit. The profit-maximising level of output occurs where $MC = MR$. This is the profit-maximising level of output as if $MR > MC$ firms could make more profit by increasing output and if $MC > MR$ firms could make more profit by reducing output. Profit-maximising firms will produce a level of output at Q_{PM} and sell at a price of P_{PM}, as illustrated on the figure.

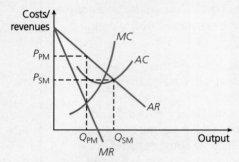

There is some evidence of this occurring in the extract. The fact that the number of models of AFVs in the market increased from 6 to 27 in such a short period of time demonstrates that firms are rapidly altering their production in response to changes in tastes and fashion, which is evidence of a firm trying to maximise profit. By switching to producing electric vehicles they will be able to take advantage of what is effectively a subsidy given by the government for these vehicles, enabling them to increase sales and for profits to rise as a consequence.

However, there is also some evidence that car manufacturers are not profit maximising. One example of this is Nissan, which is making a relatively small profit. The fact that it is investing so heavily in electric cars without much return demonstrates it may be engaging in growth maximisation. This is where its short-term objective is simply to develop market power in this growing market. This could even involve it pursuing a strategy of sales maximisation, where it produces where $AC = AR$ at Q_{SM} on the diagram above in order to generate the most sales possible. Moreover, the fact that Chery International is producing more cars than it is selling year after year is clear evidence that profit-maximising behaviour is not adopted industry wide — clearly more profit could be made by producing fewer cars.

Overall, ultimately the vast majority of car manufacturers are profit maximisers. The extent to which this is the case increases when considered from a long-term perspective — firms like Nissan may not seem motivated by profit in the short run, but they are fundamentally aiming to develop their brand in order to gain market power and make big profits in the long run. The one exception is for state-owned companies such as Chery, which are clearly not motivated by profit and are more interested in other things such as the employment their production generates. However, given state ownership is relatively small in the car industry, this does not alter the conclusion that the majority of firms are profit maximisers.

ⓔ 12/12 marks awarded. This is a very thorough answer which displays clear technical knowledge of the theory of profit maximisation and excellent evidence to support the notion that the car industry fits this theory. There is effective use of a diagram to provide further technical underpinning. The evaluation is strong as it gives a good explained example to demonstrate that not all firms in the industry are profit maximising, and goes on to offer an alternative strategy the firm might be pursuing. The judgement is well supported and displays a clear understanding of the different roles and objectives of various economic agents, recognising that state-owned companies are not profit maximisers. There is a strong link between the short- and the long-run objectives made here, enabling a successful conclusion to be reached that ultimately most car firms are profit maximisers.

Student B

(a) More new cars were purchased in 2014 than in 2010. This is because consumers are becoming more environmentally conscious and so are switching to purchasing greener vehicles.

ⓔ 1/2 marks awarded. There is recognition of the overall trend, but the statement about greener vehicles is unclear — the data should be used to demonstrate that while overall car purchases are increasing (including for traditional petrol or diesel cars), it is in the purchase of electric cars that the growth rate is strongest.

(b)

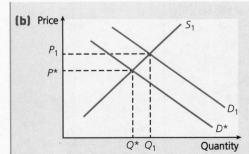

When individuals drive cars they cause several harms to the environment. The noise pollution generated, particularly by driving late at night close to residential areas, harms those local residents who are not driving but whose sleep is disrupted as a result. Moreover, the fumes emitted from the cars contribute to global warming, which harms future generations' quality of life.

ⓔ 2/4 marks awarded. The diagram illustrates negative externalities of consumption through supply and demand; for both diagram marks to be awarded a cost–benefit diagram is required. The examples of the external costs are excellent but are not linked to the diagram or to market failure — the student is missing the crucial explanation that it is because these harms are not taken into account in the market transaction that over-consumption and a welfare loss arise.

(c) Predatory pricing is taking place because firms are interdependent — i.e. the actions of one firm affect the actions of another. Therefore, when Volkswagen reduced the price of its vehicles Ford knew that consumers would switch away from them to Volkswagen if they kept their prices constant, which resulted in Ford making the decision to also cut its prices. It did this in an attempt to steal market share from Volkswagen. Such price wars demonstrate firms are acting as predators, adopting aggressive pricing strategies to try to increase their market share.

ⓔ 1/4 marks awarded. Evidence of the price changes that have taken place in the market are correctly identified but the conclusions drawn from this evidence are incorrect. The explanation would be an appropriate development of an oligopoly analysis, but the existence of inter-dependence and price wars does not mean that firms are predatory pricing. The student misunderstands the theory of predatory pricing, meaning the analysis does not answer the question set.

(d) When deciding whether an investment takes place, the government needs to consider not only the direct costs and benefits but also the costs and benefits to third parties, i.e. the externalities. Cost–benefit analysis (CBA) provides a framework through which this can be done, by adding together all the costs and benefits associated with the investment. A benefit:cost ratio can then be produced to indicate to the government which project it should invest in. For example, if the ratio was 9.3 for offering grants to individuals purchasing electric cars and 5.4 for offering grants to support the constructing of electric car charging points, this would suggest to the government that if they have a tight budget and need to cut expenditure on one project they should continue to offer grants on the electric car purchases, helping it reach the decision to no longer offer grants for the construction of charging points.

However, conducting CBA is far from straightforward — it is a time-consuming and costly process which may not be considered worthwhile in all circumstances. Even once it has been done it relies on a number of assumptions, which means a clear-cut answer is not always provided. Even if it is, the extent to which the government chooses to use this to make decisions depends upon the political climate; the government may ignore the findings from CBA and make investment decisions based upon other political concerns. For example, if the government was elected on the promise of reducing global warming it may decide to significantly increase the grants offered to support the construction of charging points, even if CBA suggests there is another project that would represent a more efficient investment.

e **4/8 marks awarded.** The analysis provides a well-worked-through example applied to the case study of how the government can use CBA to make decisions, with good use and explanation of the benefit:cost ratio. Reference to the need to assign monetary values to all costs and benefits to allow for comparisons to be made is missing. The evaluation is limited as in the main it represents a series of undeveloped statements — more technical detail is required on why CBA may struggle to produce a clear answer for the government, rather than just an explanation of why the government may just ignore whatever answer is provided.

(e) Profit maximisation occurs when the marginal cost is equal to the marginal revenue ($MC = MR$). This means that the change in total cost as a result of producing one more unit of output is equal to the change in total revenue as a result of producing one more unit of output. The fact that firms such as Volkswagen and Ford are making billions of pounds' worth of profits is evidence that they are behaving as profit maximisers, particularly as they are constantly adjusting their prices in an attempt to retain or steal customers to maximise their revenue.

However, the fact that firms such as Peugeot sell a lot of cars but make little profit is perhaps evidence that firms are not profit maximisers. The fact that they are already a leading player in the market but are not making big profits suggests there may be a degree of organisational slack present, suggesting they are not making supernormal profits. Instead those who run Peugeot may not be exhibiting maximising behaviour but are instead trying to cater for the interests of their many different stakeholders — managers want to increase sales for their own reputation, deliver some profit to shareholders to keep them in a job and keep their employees happy.

e **6/12 marks awarded.** There is a good explanation of the profit-maximising condition, which could be improved by illustrating diagrammatically. The application to the case study is good as it demonstrates that levels of profit vary depending upon the firm, but this is not in itself evidence either in support of or against the theory of profit maximisation — just because Volkswagen is making a big profit, this does not mean it is the maximum amount of profit they could possibly make. The same problem applies when the student references Peugeot not making significant profit, although the explanation that follows about the need to please many different stakeholders is reasonable as it is hinting at the concept of profit-satisficing behaviour. Reference to the principal–agent problem would be beneficial here.

■ A-level Microeconomics Section B

Quantitative essay question

In late 2015 Transport for London introduced 24-hour services on a selection of London Underground lines on Fridays and Saturdays. Unhappy with the impact this had on drivers' shift patterns, the trade unions representing these workers organised a number of strikes, where 20,000 workers refused to attend work for the day in protest over the new working arrangements. It is estimated that such strikes cost the economy £300 million a day.

Evaluate, using an appropriate diagram(s), the extent to which trade unions are responsible for labour market failure in today's economy.

(25 marks)

(e) A two-sided discussion is required here, which uses traditional diagrammatic analysis to explain how trade unions can be responsible for labour market failure. The answer should go on to consider whether the extent to which unions contribute to labour market failure has changed over time and seek examples of situations in which unions actually represent a force for good in labour markets. The answer should conclude with a supported judgement focusing on the 'extent to which' element.

Student A

Labour market failure occurs when the market forces of supply and demand do not produce an efficient allocation of resources. Trade unions can cause labour market failure by acting as the monopoly supplier of labour and using their market power to bargain for a wage rate above the equilibrium wage rate. a

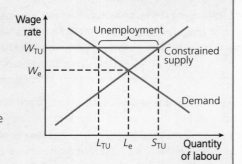

In industries where there is high union density, such as tube drivers, unions effectively operate as the monopoly supplier of labour. When entering wage negotiations they can effectively choose not to supply their labour below a target wage rate, meaning firms are forced to pay a wage rate of W_{TU}, as illustrated in the diagram below, which is above the equilibrium wage rate of W_e. This represents labour market failure because workers are being paid above the market clearing wage and it also creates inequality of income between those who are members of unions and those who aren't — evidence of a union 'mark-up' still exists in the labour market today, with tube drivers earning approximately £50,000. The threat of the strike is what enables them to achieve such high wages. b

Moreover, the existence of trade unions can cause unemployment. Because firms are forced to pay higher wages for workers, their costs of production rise as a consequence and they may choose to lay off workers, reducing employment below the equilibrium level to $L*$. In fact, the existence of trade unions can significantly reduce the flexibility of labour markets, as firms find it more difficult to alter tasks and hours of workers and as a consequence may be discouraged from hiring workers in the first place. c

However, while it is clear that unions are still responsible for labour market failure, there is strong evidence that the extent to which this is the case has been declining in recent years. This is largely because unions have experienced declining bargaining power as a result of a changing industrial structure in the UK economy. The UK economy has deindustrialised and moved towards tertiary sector employment, which is historically less unionised. In fact, in many service sector firms the emergence of professional human resources departments, who deal with many of the employee relations issues previously handled by unions, has meant the role of the union has become increasingly marginalised, further decreasing the number of people joining unions. Because the service sector has a low percentage of the workforce belonging to unions, this has reduced the bargaining power of trade unions, limiting the extent to which they caused labour market failure in 2015. d

In response to this declining bargaining power, some argue unions have adapted their role and increasingly act in ways which improve, rather than hinder, the efficiency of labour markets. Many unions now act in a consultative manner, acting as a middle man between employee and employer to communicate to firms workers' concerns and ideas to improve the productivity of the firm. Moreover, some unions have realised that the way to increase the wages of their workers and secure their jobs in the long term is through encouraging their workers to become more productive. To this end unions have begun running training courses to improve worker productivity, raising the marginal revenue product of workers and as a result improving the efficiency of labour markets. e

Moreover, there are many instances in which in negotiating higher wages unions have a positive impact on labour markets today. Given that unions don't have a significant impact on the labour market in many industries, many of the industries in which they are powerful are actually situations of monopsony. This is where firms are the monopoly buyer of labour. In such instances firms without union intervention would act in a way which results in labour market failure, as they are able to use their monopoly power to set wages below the equilibrium wage of $W*$ at W_M and restrict employment to L_M, as illustrated in the diagram below. They do this because the marginal cost of employing an additional worker is very high, as they will have to pay not only the new worker a higher wage but raise the wage of all existing employees. The result is that they restrict employment below the labour market equilibrium and pay workers significantly below their *MRP*, resulting in labour market failure. Because the firm is the monopoly buyer of labour, workers simply have to accept these low wages as there is no other employer demanding their labour. Under such circumstances unions help correct labour market failure by operating in a situation of bilateral monopoly. As a monopoly seller of labour, unions can set a minimum wage at which there will be no supply of labour below it. If they set this close to the competitive equilibrium wage it will result in wages and employment rising to W_{TU} and L_{TU} respectively. This results in the labour market becoming more efficient, as the market power of unions effectively counteracts the market power of the monopsonist and ensures the worker is not exploited. [f]

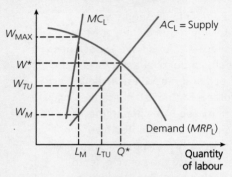

In judgement, it is clear that in the majority of industries unions are not a significant cause of labour market failure. Decline in union power and the increasing importance of industries which are not heavily unionised mean other forms of labour market failure are more important in today's economy. However, while the breadth of impact is perhaps limited, the significant impact unions are able to have on some industries remains. Given we operate in an increasingly price-competitive international marketplace, one could argue unions now more than ever could cause labour market failure, as raising costs of firms by too much could ultimately lead to firms relocating abroad or being outcompeted by foreign competition, resulting in large-scale unemployment as a consequence. [g]

e **23/25 marks awarded.** [a] The answer starts by demonstrating good knowledge and understanding of what is meant by labour market failure. [b] There is an accurate diagram illustrating the impact of union wage bargaining on the labour market, which is supported by an explanation of why this represents labour market failure. [c] The analysis is then well developed to explain other ways in which trade unions contribute to labour market failure. More could have been said about the power and impact of a strike, as this in itself represents a major economic harm caused by trade unions. [d] Strong evaluation is offered, presenting a number of reasons why the influence of unions has been declining and therefore resulting in them causing less labour market failure. [e] The argument that unions actually reduce labour market failure through improving workers' productivity is well made, although it would be strengthened by the inclusion of a productivity bargaining diagram. [f] The bilateral monopoly argument is presented superbly, with an accurate diagram further illustrating why unions are not always the harmful agents one might think them to be. [g] A clear judgement is reached, recognising that while unions are less pervasive than in previous decades, their ability to cause significant problems in some labour markets remains unchanged. Throughout, the answer would have benefited from more examples of specific labour markets to bring the technical theory to life.

Student B

Unions continue to cause labour market failure by reducing labour market flexibility. One reason they exist is to protect workers' conditions and rights. This makes it difficult for firms to alter the way in which they employ workers to improve efficiency — for example, London Underground may like to vary the working hours or shift patterns of its drivers but is unable to because it fears a union backlash. Supply of labour is therefore more elastic, causing labour market failure as shown below. **a**

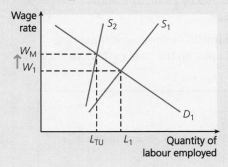

Unions also cause labour market failure because they lead to lost output. When tube drivers went on strike it meant that many people who rely on the tube to get to work were not able to go. This could cause negative economic growth and harm the balance of payments. **b**

However, anti-union legislation means unions do not cause labour market failure any more. In the 1980s a range of legislation was introduced to reduce the power of unions, such as the introduction of compulsory strike ballots. This reduced the ability of unions to cause significant unexpected disruption to firms, as the process of conducting a ballot is time consuming and provides the employer time to either try to resolve the dispute or prepare contingency plans to cope when its workers strike. This has reduced the effectiveness of strikes and, along with other anti-union legislation such as the ban on second-line picketing, has resulted in the number of strike days falling dramatically. **c**

e **7/25 marks awarded.** **a** The student correctly identifies that trade unions can cause the labour market to become less flexible and illustrates this using a diagram showing the supply of labour becoming more inelastic. This is a reasonable approach, but the diagram is not then explained, meaning it is unclear what, if any, labour market failure results from this. **b** The harms a strike can cause to the economy are considered, but this is not well explained — there is an assertion about the negative impact on the balance of payments without a clear chain of analysis. **c** The evaluation is reasonable as the student provides a clear explanation of why the power of unions has been declining, but they do not go on to explain why this consequently means unions are now less responsible for labour market failure. No judgement is offered and the 'extent to which' element of the question has been ignored.

■A-level Microeconomics Section C

Qualitative essay question

Since 2010 the government has been increasing the personal tax allowance, rising from £6,475 to a targeted £12,500 by 2020. In 2015 the government also announced plans to increase the income level at which individuals start paying the higher rate of tax from £42,385 in 2015 to £50,000 by 2020. One of the objectives of this was to improve incentives to work.

Evaluate the extent to which the income and substitution effects are important determinants of labour supply and the impact this has on the likely effectiveness of the government's tax reforms. (25 marks)

Student A

In the short run, there is insufficient time for workers to move between jobs and for firms to hire new workers, meaning labour supply is determined on the basis of individual decisions about working hours. When deciding how many hours to work individuals are effectively making a choice between work and leisure — there are a limited number of hours in a day and they need to decide whether to work more hours (earning a higher income at the cost of less leisure time) or to reduce their working hours (enjoying more leisure time at the cost of a lower income). These decisions are determined by the income and substitution effects. a

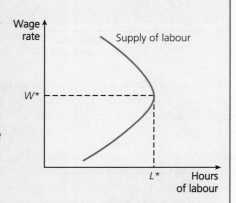

As wages increase, all individuals experience a substitution effect. As wages increase, the opportunity cost of leisure increases, as you are having to sacrifice more money that you could have earned if you were working. This incentivises individuals to substitute leisure for labour in order for them to take advantage of the higher wages on offer. Individuals also experience an income effect. Leisure is a normal good with a positive income elasticity of demand. Therefore, as wages rise, demand for leisure increases, meaning individuals are incentivised to reduce their working hours in order to consume more leisure. Clearly, the income and substitution effects present a conflicting explanation of what happens to individual labour supply when the wage rate changes. b

The strength of the income and substitution effects depends upon the wage level of the individual. As shown above, at low wages below W^* the substitution effect is thought to dominate. The substitution effect is large because individuals on low income feel a big incentive to work more hours when the wage rate rises as it enables them to significantly enhance their material standard of living. The income effect is relatively small as at low incomes individuals cannot afford particularly good quality leisure activities, meaning they do not value leisure that highly. Therefore at low wages an increase in the wage rate is likely to increase the quantity of labour supplied.

The reverse is true at high wages above W^* in the diagram above. Here the substitution effect is relatively small — individuals already have sufficient income to enjoy a high material standard of living and are already likely to have 'excess' income that they are saving. The income effect is likely to be large as high-earning individuals really value extra leisure time because they can afford to engage in high-quality leisure pursuits. Therefore, above a wage of W^*, labour supply decreases as the wage rate increases. c

This has clear implications for the success of the government's tax policies outlined in the question. Given that those most affected by increases in the personal allowance will be individuals on low incomes, it is likely that increasing this will cause an increase in labour supply. Knowing they can keep more of their post-tax income effectively represents an increase in the wage rate and this will incentivise those at the bottom of the income distribution to increase their working hours. However, raising the threshold at which individuals pay the higher rate of income tax may actually cause labour supply to fall. Such individuals are already earning a relatively high income and so may experience a large income effect when their post-tax income increases, causing a contraction in labour supply. d

However, in reality there are a number of limiting factors which suggest that the income and substitution effects are perhaps less significant determinants of labour supply than first thought. This is because in most jobs individuals have fixed contracted hours which cannot easily be altered — workers rarely in practice have the opportunity to adjust the number of hours they work. This therefore means that the income and substitution effects are not seen in operation in many real-world labour markets. Moreover, the suggestion that the government's policy of raising the threshold at which you pay the higher rate of tax will result in labour supply falling depends upon the exact value of W^*; it could be argued that an individual earning £45,000 supporting a family does not have sufficiently high income to be on the backward-bending portion of the labour supply curve, meaning the substitution effect may still dominate the income effect at this level of income. e

Also in the long run, people can move between occupations and firms can hire new workers, meaning there are other, more significant determinants of labour supply. For example, some jobs require particular qualifications or skills which are essential to being able to carry out the job. Suppose there was a shortage of computer engineers. Even if the wage rate increased and there was a big substitution effect (i.e. an unemployed individual was really incentivised to enter the labour market), there would be very little increase in the supply of labour because most individuals not already supplying their labour as computer engineers simply wouldn't have the appropriate skills. Equally, in jobs that are vocational in nature the income and substitution effects are not important determinants of labour supply. This is because labour supply in industries such as nursing is not determined by the wage but by the love of the job — changes in the wage would cause very little change in labour supply. If such non-pecuniary factors are crucial determinants of labour supply it is unlikely that government policy designed to influence labour supply by changing the wage rate will be effective. [f]

In conclusion, while the income and substitution effects are likely to be important determinants of labour supply in the short run, in the long run it is more likely that the non-pecuniary factors which determine long-run labour supply and the elasticity of labour supply are more significant determinants of labour supply. [g]

ⓔ 21/25 marks awarded. [a] The student quickly identifies that the income and substitution effects are relevant in the short run. [b] There is a strong explanation of the income and substitution effects and the fact that both effects are experienced to an extent by all individuals is correctly identified. [c] An outstanding technical analysis is presented of how the relative size of the income and substitution effect changes depending upon the wage rate. [d] This is then well applied to analyse the likely impact of reforms to the government's income tax policy. [e] There is strong evaluation, which presents a number of criticisms of the theory associated with the income and substitution effect. [f] The student effectively illustrates how other factors could potentially be more significant determinants of labour supply and links this back to the likely impact of government policy. [g] While the judgement makes a clear distinction between the short run and the long run, it is unsubstantiated and does not link back to the policy element in the question.

Student B

At low wages there is a significant substitution effect. This is because individuals on low income really want extra money, so when the wage rate increases they want to work more hours in order to raise their income. The monetary benefits on offer in a low-wage occupation tend to be a significant motivating factor determining the supply of labour. At high wages there is a significant income effect. This is because when wages increase individuals are incentivised to reduce their working hours to maintain the same income level and in doing so give them more time to undertake leisure activities. [a]

For example, suppose a waitress was offered an increase in the hourly wage rate from £7 to £8. This is likely to cause her to increase labour supply and work more hours, as she is probably working to earn some spending money and would really value a higher income. Whereas when an accountant earns £150 an hour and is offered a wage increase to £200, they are more likely to decide to work fewer hours now they are paid more per hour to generate more leisure time. [b] The government policies are likely to be effective in increasing labour supply as they are likely to increase the size of the substitution effect. [c]

However, there are a number of other factors which also determine labour supply, such as the pleasantness of the job. Labour supply of refuse collection workers is relatively low despite the reasonable wage they earn because most individuals are unwilling to supply their labour to this occupation. This is because it is unpleasant handling rubbish and potentially involves some danger when loading bin lorries on a busy road. Labour supply would be much higher at any given wage rate for stewards at football matches, who enjoy the job because it means they get to experience the atmosphere and perhaps see some of the game.

Another factor which determines labour supply is promotion prospects. Some individuals, such as trainee lawyers, may be willing to supply their labour at relatively low wage rates in comparison to their skill level because they are attracted by the potential of earning high wages in the future. Labour supply of a teacher is likely to be lower at any given wage rate because teachers are less likely to see their salaries grow at the same rate as lawyers. d

e **12/25 marks awarded.** a The explanation of the income and substitution effect is good, but the conflict between the two is not clearly explained; the student should recognise that both effects are present at all levels of income but it is the strength of them that varies according to the wage. b The examples effectively bring the concepts to life, but more technical rigour is needed, which could be achieved by including a diagram. c The student explains the impact government tax reforms are likely to have on the substitution effect but does not go on to develop this analysis sufficiently. d The answer then moves on to present a good explanation with clear examples of two alternative factors that determine labour supply, but this evaluation is reasonable only because these factors are not weighed up against the income and substitution effect or made relevant to the government policies proposed in the question. The answer lacks a supported judgement.

■ A-level Themes in Economics Section A

Multiple choice

Question 1

The environmental Kuznets curve illustrates:

A   The negative externalities caused to the environment by production

B   The depletion of natural resources over time

C   The relationship between environmental degradation and economic growth

D   The divergence between social and private marginal cost

Question 2

The average revenue curve will be perfectly elastic in the model of:

A   Perfect competition

B   Monopolistic competition

C   Oligopoly

D   Monopoly

Question 3

Assuming *ceteris paribus*, wage rates are likely to be highest when:

A   Supply of labour is high and inelastic

B   Supply of labour is low and elastic

C   Demand for labour is high and elastic

D   Supply of and demand for labour are high

Question 4

Which of the following correctly describes the monopsony outcome?

Option	Quantity of labour employed (compared with competitive equilibrium)	Wage rate (compared with competitive equilibrium)
A	Higher	Higher
B	Lower	Lower
C	Higher	Lower
D	Lower	Higher

Question 5

A public sector firm is most likely to be pursuing the objective of:

A Profit maximisation

B Revenue maximisation

C Profit satisficing

D Utility maximisation

Answers and rationale

Question 1

A Some production will cause environmental negative externalities, but this is illustrated using a cost–benefit diagram.

B While natural resources are depleting over time, this is not illustrated by the Kuznets curve.

C *Correct answer.* Initially environmental degradation increases with economic growth but then starts to decrease as countries move into more advanced stages of economic development.

D When there are negative externalities present there will be a divergence between social and private cost, but this is not shown on the Kuznets curve.

Question 2

A *Correct answer.* In perfect competition firms are price takers and are too small to influence the market price, meaning they face infinite demand at the given price level.

B The demand curve is reasonably price elastic in monopolistic competition because there are lots of substitutes, but the fact that products are differentiated means firms have a degree of market power and the demand curve is not perfectly elastic.

C The interdependence of firms means the demand curve is kinked in the model of oligopoly.

D Monopoly firms are the dominant supplier of the product and so have significant market power and an inelastic demand curve.

Question 3

A *Correct answer.* When supply of labour is inelastic workers require significant increases in the wage to supply their labour to an occupation, perhaps because of the training required. The limited supply also means firms are in fierce competition for workers, pushing up the wage rate.

B When supply of labour is elastic firms need to raise the wage rate by only a small amount to encourage a big increase in the quantity of labour supplied, meaning they do not need to pay high wages to attract workers. When labour supply is plentiful there is less competition for workers, which also pushes wages down.

C A high demand for labour will mean workers generate significant revenue for firms, incentivising high wages. However, when the demand for labour is elastic firms have high bargaining power, perhaps because labour can be easily substituted for capital, pushing wage rates down.

D The plentiful supply of labour will push wage rates down, offsetting the impact of a high demand for labour and meaning wages will be lower than in option A.

Question 4

A Firms will not pay workers above the competitive equilibrium as they can exploit their market power as the sole buyer of labour. They will not employ more workers than in the competitive equilibrium as keeping employment low enables them to keep wages low — the marginal cost of labour is particularly high in a monopsony.

B *Correct answer.* Firms employ workers where the marginal revenue product of labour equals the marginal cost of labour, which delivers an equilibrium below the competitive equilibrium. Firms then pay a wage rate on the labour supply curve, below the competitive equilibrium.

C Firms restrict employment below the competitive equilibrium to keep wage rates low.

D Firms can pay workers below the competitive equilibrium because there are no other firms workers can supply their labour to.

Question 5

A A public sector firm is run by the government, which is not incentivised by profit.

B Public sector firms often provide their goods and services for free or certainly below competitive equilibrium prices, demonstrating they are not aiming to maximise revenue.

C Profit satisficing is more common in large public limited companies with many different stakeholders to please.

D *Correct answer.* Public sector firms tend to exist to provide a good-quality service/access to the service to the general population — maximising service users' welfare therefore tends to be the primary objective.

■ A-level Themes in Economics Section B

Data-response

The UK labour market has changed dramatically over the past 50 years. Globalisation has contributed to rapid deindustrialisation and permanently altered the structure of employment in the UK, with the proportion of the workforce employed in the service sector doubling to more than 80% in 2015. The age profile of the labour force is also changing, with the ageing population contributing to an ageing workforce which is only likely to get older as the retirement age increases in the coming years. Charts 3 and 4 provide further information on changes in the UK labour market, focusing on the role of part-time employment and how unemployment rates vary by age group.

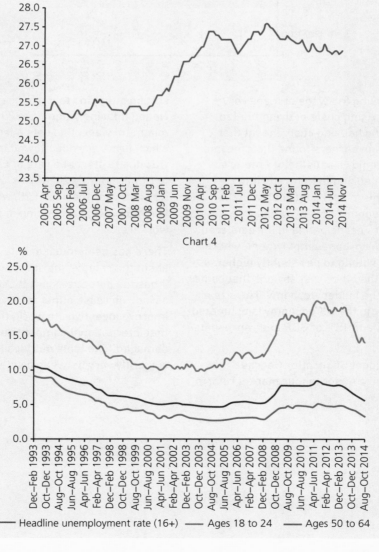

Chart 3

Chart 4

Headline unemployment rate (16+) — Ages 18 to 24 — Ages 50 to 64

Fierce international competition combined with the existence of many relatively low-skilled service sector jobs resulted in many workers earning wages that were insufficient to keep them out of poverty, putting pressure on the government to top up their income with a range of means-tested benefits. To try to address this problem the government introduced a National Minimum Wage in 1999, setting a floor on wages below which it became illegal to employ workers. Chart 5 illustrates how the minimum wage has evolved since then to reach the £6.50 an hour the full adult rate stood at in 2015, paid to all workers aged 21 and over.

Chart 5

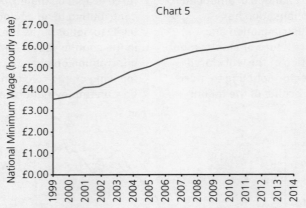

Despite initially raising the wage of many very low-paid workers, rising costs of living fuelled by rapidly increasing housing costs meant that many minimum wage earners found their income was insufficient to enjoy a satisfactory material standard of living, causing them to slip into relative poverty. This in part contributed to the rise in informal economic activity, with increasing numbers of workers participating in unregistered or unrecorded cash-in-hand employment, where employers may be willing to pay slightly higher wages because of the other cost savings that come from operating in the hidden economy. The size of the informal sector in the UK economy is estimated to be between 10% and 15% of GDP and represents untaxed output.

In the July 2015 Budget Chancellor George Osborne announced a major labour market reform, setting out plans to introduce a compulsory National Living Wage from 2016. Much like the minimum wage, this sets a legal minimum below which firms are not allowed to employ workers. It was due to start at a rate of £7.20 per hour, rising to £9 per hour by 2020. This will apply only to workers over the age of 25, with the lower National Minimum Wage remaining in place for younger workers.

There has been much debate among economists about the relative merits of such a policy. While it has the potential to lift those who experience a wage increase out of relative poverty and improve incentives to work, there are concerns that international competitiveness will be badly damaged. The table outlines how minimum wages currently vary between a selection of countries.

Country	National Minimum Wage (USD)	National Minimum Wage as a percentage of average income
Australia	30,791	5.00%
Brazil	4,341	39.80%
Ecuador	4,956	80.80%
Germany	23,750	48.20%
India	603	42.40%
UK	21,246	43.70%
USA	15,080	28.40%

One group of workers that looks certain to benefit from the National Living Wage is those involved in social care, with 700,000 care workers, many of whom are currently paid the National Minimum Wage, likely to see significant increases in their pay. To an extent this could be seen to be correcting the labour market failure that results from the government exploiting its monopsony power in this sector, although this is likely to come at a cost of £2 billion to already stretched government finances.

(a) State two factors that determine the demand for labour. (2 marks)

ⓔ Identify two factors of demand, considering the theory of the marginal revenue product of labour. This question does not require you to explain any of the factors.

(b) Using Charts 3 and 4, identify trends in the UK labour market. (2 marks)

ⓔ Look for the overall change that has taken place in both charts and explain what this change shows. Aim to support both trends you identify by quoting evidence from the data.

(c) In July 2015 the Chancellor announced the introduction of a National Living Wage. Using an appropriate diagram, explain the impact of moving from a National Minimum Wage to a National Living Wage. (4 marks)

ⓔ Draw a labour market diagram clearly illustrating how competitive labour markets are affected by a move from a minimum to a living wage. Use this diagram to explain the impact on wages and employment and any wider consequences of this.

(d) Evaluate whether imposing a National Living Wage is likely to reduce informal labour market activity. (8 marks)

ⓔ The directive word 'evaluate' means a two-sided answer is required here. Offer at least one developed analytical point explaining why informal labour market activity might fall as a result of the National Living Wage being imposed followed by at least one argument on the other side explaining why informal labour market activity might stay the same or rise. The answer should end with a clearly supported judgement explaining what you think will happen to informal labour market activity as a result of the National Living Wage being introduced.

(e) Evaluate the extent to which the imposition of a National Living Wage will harm the UK's international competitiveness. (15 marks)

ⓔ A two-sided answer is required here which recognises the harms a National Living Wage could cause to international competitiveness while considering reasons why these harms may not be particularly significant. You could also consider why international competitiveness may actually improve as a result of this policy. Be sure to explain what is meant by international competitiveness within your answer and conclude by providing a supported judgement that is clearly focused on the question.

(f) With reference to the data in Table 1, compare the differences in the minimum wages which can be seen between countries. (4 marks)

ⓔ Seek to identify differences between the raw minimum wages between countries and then see whether the country rankings are the same when comparing the minimum wage as a percentage of average income. Make sure you quote the data in your answer.

(g) Using an appropriate diagram, evaluate the extent to which prior to the introduction of a National Living Wage care workers were paid low wages because the government acted as a monopsonist employer. (15 marks)

ⓔ Start by analysing how the government could be seen to be a monopsony employer in the care workers industry. Use a monopsony diagram to evidence the wage rate that was paid by the government. Evaluate your analysis by recognising its limitations and the conditions under which it might not hold, before reaching a supported judgement where you clearly explain whether or not you believe the government acted as a monopsonist employer.

Student A
(a) Productivity of workers and the price of the product.

ⓔ 2/2 marks awarded. The student successfully identifies the two components of the marginal revenue product of labour — productivity is the marginal physical product of labour (MPP) and the price of the product reflects the marginal revenue (MR) in a perfectly competitive market.

(b) Part-time employment has increased from 25.3% of the workforce in 2005 to 27.0% of the workforce in 2014. The youth unemployment rate has been above the headline unemployment rate throughout the period but the gap between the two has increased.

ⓔ 2/2 marks awarded. The trend of rising part-time employment has been correctly identified and the data quoted effectively to support this. Spotting that youth unemployment remains higher than the headline unemployment rate throughout the period but that the gap between the two has increased demonstrates an excellent understanding of the trend being illustrated here.

(c)

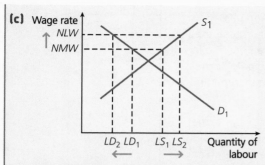

Moving from a National Minimum Wage to a National Living Wage essentially has the impact of raising the wage rate further above the competitive equilibrium wage rate. This is illustrated in the diagram above, with the wage rate increasing from *NMW* to *NLW*. This is likely to reduce relative poverty as individuals on low pay find they are able to afford a better material standard of living.

ⓔ 3/4 marks awarded. The student presents an accurate diagram which recognises that transitioning to a National Living Wage can essentially be modelled as an increase in the National Minimum Wage. The explanation demonstrates an understanding that a living wage might reduce poverty, but there is no reference to the x-axis on the diagram, which clearly shows unemployment rising as a result of the policy. There also could have been mention of the fact that the National Living Wage will have no direct impact on those over 21 but under the age of 25, who will continue to receive the National Minimum Wage.

(d) Prior to the introduction of the National Living Wage, it is likely that many workers felt forced into working in the informal economy because the formal economy was not offering them a sufficiently high wage to enjoy what they deemed to be an acceptable standard of living. Individuals therefore sought work for firms that were willing to pay cash in hand and keep their employment off the books. Some employers will be willing to pay workers higher wages under such circumstances because they can avoid paying other costs associated with employing workers, such as national insurance contributions. The introduction of the living wage incentivises workers into the formal sector, as the wages offered there are now high enough to maintain an acceptable standard of living. Even though wages may still be higher in the informal sector for the reasons previously explained, most workers if given the choice would rather work in the formal economy because such jobs offer them a number of rights they would not get in the informal economy, such as holiday entitlement and sick pay. The transition of people from the informal to the formal economy is therefore likely to reduce informal labour market activity.

However, this depends upon the tax and benefits system in place. If taxes on low-income individuals are high then even with a high living wage individuals might still be incentivised to operate in the informal economy, as working in the formal economy still provides them with too little post-tax income because of the amount of their income they have to give to the government in the form of taxation. Moreover, if individuals lose their entitlement to means-tested benefits as they begin to earn an income in the labour market, many might remain incentivised to participate in the informal economy to enable them to simultaneously earn an income and claim benefits.

Overall it is likely that implementing the living wage will reduce informal labour market activity, particularly because the government introduced the policy at a time when it was raising the personal income tax allowance, creating further incentive for individuals to operate in the formal economy.

📝 **7/8 marks awarded.** There is a strong analysis of the reasons why individuals participate in the informal economy and why such incentives are likely to be reduced as a result of the implementation of a National Living Wage. The evaluation is also strong, recognising that the nature of the tax and benefits system could still encourage some individuals to remain in the informal economy. The judgement is well supported as it recognises that the National Living Wage was introduced as part of an overall policy framework which should reduce informal labour market activity. The only thing missing from this answer is any consideration of why informal labour market activity might actually increase as a result of the introduction of the National Living Wage.

(e) Introducing a National Living Wage is likely to raise firms' costs of production. Labour costs are for many firms the most significant component of costs of production, meaning when labour costs rise a firm's costs of production may increase significantly. This will cause the supply curve to shift to the left and raise the price of the good. a As illustrated in Table 1, the UK already has a relatively high minimum wage in comparison with other countries. By effectively raising this through introducing a National Living Wage, this may make UK firms' costs of production significantly higher than those of firms in other nations, causing the price of UK goods and services to rise at a faster rate than in other countries. This will cause UK goods and services to become relatively less price competitive. b As price is one of the major factors firms compete on, this could cause a fall in demand for UK goods and services, with consumers switching to purchase goods and services from relatively cheaper foreign suppliers who do not have to pay such high wages. c

However, the extent to which introducing a National Living Wage is harmful to international competitiveness depends upon whether productivity improves as a consequence. Given workers are now being paid higher wages it may incentivise them to work harder and produce more output, while firms might also be incentivised to invest more in training workers given they are having to pay them higher wages. This could lead to both the quality and quantity of output increasing, which could improve international competitiveness. d Moreover, it should be noted that the cost of employing all workers has not increased — those aged under 25 will remain on the

National Minimum Wage. Therefore, those firms which employ younger workers will not necessarily see their international competitiveness harmed. In fact, this policy change may encourage firms to seek to employ younger workers, which could help to reduce the high youth unemployment rate. e

Ultimately, while raising firms' costs of production in a globalised and internationally price-competitive environment could initially seem very harmful, the National Living Wage is unlikely to significantly hurt the UK's international competitiveness. Most workers who will benefit from this are in service sector occupations such as hairdressing which are not subject to international competition, while the financial services sector (the area in which the UK has the most substantial comparative advantage) will be largely unaffected. It is only in a few industries where problems might arise, such as car manufacturing, where MNCs are likely to react by relocating production to lower-labour-cost countries. f

e **15/15 marks awarded.** a The student offers a correct technical explanation of why the price of UK goods and services is likely to rise as a result of the National Living Wage being implemented. b The stimulus material is used effectively to demonstrate why this might be a particular problem for UK firms. c Strong analysis is then offered to explain the damage this will do to the international competitiveness of domestic firms. d Strong evaluation is presented which recognises the potentially positive impact a National Living Wage can have on productivity. e The idea that the policy may help to reduce youth unemployment provides further evidence of the merits of a National Living Wage. f The answer ends with an excellent supported judgement which provides strong argumentation as to why the National Living Wage is ultimately unlikely to cause significant harm to the UK's international competitiveness.

(f) The national minimum wage is highest in Australia and lowest in India — it is $30,188 higher in Australia. Countries which have the highest minimum wages do not necessarily have the highest minimum wage as a proportion of average incomes in the country — an example of this is the USA, which has the third highest annual minimum wage of the countries presented here ($15,080) but the lowest minimum wage as a percentage of average income (28.40%).

e **3/4 marks awarded.** A valid comparison is made between the minimum wage levels in Australia and India with a correct calculation to demonstrate the size of this difference. The point about the discrepancies between the two sets of data is well made but could be more developed, either by explaining why this pattern exists (the USA is a high-wage country, so it is unsurprising that its minimum wage is significantly higher than a country such as India, but that this represents a smaller proportion of average income) or by comparing this to a country such as Ecuador, with a relatively low absolute minimum wage but which represents a high proportion of average income.

(g) A monopsonist is the sole buyer of labour in a labour market. In the care sector the vast majority of care workers are employed by the government. **a** Unlike employers operating in a perfectly competitive labour market, who are wage takers and simply employ workers at the going wage rate, monopsonists face the industry labour supply curve directly. Because they are the monopoly buyer of labour, the number of workers they employ influences the wage rate — the only way to employ more workers is to increase the wage rate, which is why the supply curve is upward sloping. As shown in the diagram below, the MC_L curve is steeper than the AC_L curve because it is particularly expensive to hire additional care workers — the change in total cost as a result of employing one more unit of labour reflects the fact that the cost of hiring an additional unit of labour not only involved the wage paid to that worker, but also the increase in the wages paid to all other workers because of the increase in the equilibrium wage rate. **b**

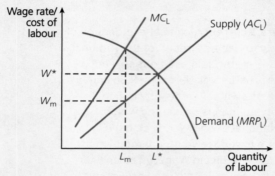

Assuming that the government behaves as a profit maximiser, it will determine the quantity of labour it will employ by the profit-maximising condition $MRP_L = MC_L$. Equilibrium in a monopsony will not be reached when $MRP_L \rightarrow MC_L$ because the change in total revenue resulting from employing one more unit of labour will exceed the change in total cost resulting from employing one more unit of labour, meaning more profit could be made by employing more workers. Equally, the government would not be profit maximising when $MC_L \rightarrow MRP_L$, as the change in total cost resulting from employing the last unit of labour would exceed the change in total revenue resulting from employing the last unit of labour, meaning a greater profit can be made by reducing the number of workers employed. This means the government will employ L_m care workers, where $MRP_L = MC_L$, i.e. the change in total revenue resulting from employing one more unit of labour is exactly equal to the change in total cost from employing one more unit of labour. **c**

The wage rate of W_m will be below the competitive equilibrium wage rate of W^*. This is the lowest wage the government is able to pay to generate enough labour supply to produce the profit-maximising level of output. This represents labour market failure as workers are paid significantly below their MRP_L and provides a powerful argument to explain why care workers were paid low wages before the introduction of the National Living Wage. The government was effectively able to exploit workers in this way because of the market power it holds — care workers are unable to move to another firm to earn a higher wage because the monopsonist is the only firm in the market, enabling them to sustain low wages. In this sense, then, the National Living Wage could be seen as important in correcting labour market failure. d

However, this analysis is based on the crucial assumption that the government acts as a profit maximiser. This is unrealistic because the government does not seek to profit from healthcare provision (it doesn't charge anything to consumers for its use) and instead seeks to maximise social welfare by ensuring as many people as possible have access to high-quality care provision. Therefore, even though the government has the potential to act as a monopsonist by setting wages below the competitive equilibrium wage, it is unlikely to do so because it is not motivated by profit. e

Instead, traditional labour market theory can be used to explain why care workers earn low wages. Because they are relatively low skilled their supply of labour is elastic and plentiful, while the relatively small number of patients they can look after at a time (who are incidentally not paying for the service) means that the marginal revenue product of labour is also low. These factors combined explain why care workers earn relatively low wages; the National Living Wage therefore has the potential to distort this labour market by pushing the wages of care workers above the competitive equilibrium. f

Overall, then, it is unlikely that care workers earn low wages because the government was exploiting its power as a monopsonist because the government has no incentive to restrict employment and pay low wages as it is not aiming to maximise profits. g

e **11/15 marks awarded.** a The answer begins by clearly explaining what is meant by a monopsonist and identifying what that means in the context of the social care sector. b There is an accurate diagram which is well explained, with strong analysis of why the marginal cost of labour exceeds the average cost of labour. c This is supported by strong analysis of the profit-maximising condition to explain the quantity of labour employed in a monopsony. d By explaining the impact this model has on wages the student is able to provide strong evidence to demonstrate that care workers were essentially underpaid because of the government's monopsony power. e The evaluation is strong because it recognises the fundamental flaw in the model — that the government is a profit maximiser. The student goes on to explain why this means it is unlikely that the government exploits its monopsony power by paying low wages. f An alternative reason for the low wages earned by care workers is provided and well explained. g A supported judgement is offered, although this is very weak, simply repeating a point offered earlier in the answer.

Questions & Answers

(a) Government tax policy and derived demand.

e **1/2 marks awarded.** Government tax policy will affect the demand for labour because if the government reduces employer national insurance contributions this effectively reduces the cost of employing workers, thus increasing the demand for labour. Derived demand is an explanation of what the demand for labour is rather than a determinant of it — the student would have needed to write 'demand for the product' to be awarded a mark for this point.

(b) The percentage of workers in part-time employment has increased. The youth unemployment rate is significantly higher than the headline unemployment rate.

e **1/2 marks awarded.** The student correctly identifies the trend of the increased contribution part-time employment is making to the labour market. Specific reference to the data — i.e. the percentage of workers in part-time employment increased by 1.7% between 2005 and 2014 — would have enabled the second mark to be awarded. The second statement does not identify a trend but simply the relationship between the youth and adult unemployment rates.

(c)

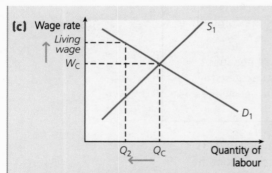

Imposing a living wage will cause the wage rate to increase from W_c to *Living wage*. While this is good for workers it does have the impact of causing unemployment, as some firms lay off workers as they are unwilling to pay the higher wage rate — there is a contraction along the labour demand curve from Q_c to Q_2.

e **2/4 marks awarded.** The diagram correctly illustrates the impact of imposing a floor wage above the competitive equilibrium but ignores the transition element of the question — this diagram suggests a living wage is being imposed in a labour market without previous intervention, ignoring the existence of a minimum wage. The student makes good reference to the unemployment generated by a living wage and could develop this by explaining that as well as the contraction along the labour demand curve there will be an extension along the labour supply curve, further contributing to unemployment.

(d) Informal economic activity is likely to rise, not fall, as a result of the National Living Wage being imposed. This is because firms faced with higher labour costs may reduce the number of workers they employ, causing unemployment. These individuals who are displaced from the formal sector may be forced to look for work in the informal labour market. Moreover, firms facing higher costs of production may be tempted to try to reduce these costs by employing workers in the informal economy, where they can pay a wage below the National Living Wage. Therefore, because the National Living Wage will incentivise both workers and firms to engage in informal employment, informal labour market activity is likely to increase.

ⓔ 3/8 marks awarded. There is a reasonable analysis on one side of the argument, explaining why rising costs of production caused by the National Living Wage could mean informal labour market activity increases. However, the answer lacks a consideration of the other side — there needs to be some explanation as to why informal labour market activity may fall.

(e) The rise in wage rates that will result from moving from a National Minimum Wage to a National Living Wage will force firms to pass on these higher wages to consumers in the form of higher prices. This causes both domestic and foreign consumers to find UK goods less attractive. This will cause demand for UK goods and services to fall and demand for foreign goods and services to rise, which will worsen the balance of payments and cause unemployment. a

However, it is unlikely to cause significant harm to UK firms because in the areas in which they are involved in international competition they have a significant comparative advantage which will not be diminished by rising wage costs. Labour costs are also not the only costs in the production process; the UK has much capital-intensive production, which will be largely unaffected by rising wage costs. b

ⓔ 6/15 marks awarded. a The student offers good analysis explaining why the price of UK goods and services is likely to rise, although a more explicit link to costs of production would be beneficial. There is good reference to the macroeconomic objectives that will be affected by the National Living Wage, but there is a lack of focused analysis on the direct impact on international competitiveness — the importance of price competitiveness must be considered. b The evaluation is reasonable. While the reference to the importance of comparative advantage is valid and the statement that capital-intensive production will be unaffected is valid, more specific detail needs to be provided to bring this to life. The answer lacks a supported judgement.

(f) The national minimum wage is highest in Australia and lowest in India. Ecuador's minimum wage is the highest as a percentage of GDP per capita; the USA has the lowest minimum wage on this measure.

ⓔ **2/4 marks awarded.** Both statements are correct direct interpretations of the data presented. The answer does need to include specific reference to figures in the data, though, while some more analytical comparisons (such as comparing the different rankings of countries between the two data sets) would enable the student to access the higher marks.

(g) The government is the only employer of care workers and so is able to exploit its market power, as shown in the diagram below.

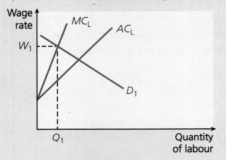

Because care workers will not be able to find employment working for any other firm, since the government is the only firm employing care workers, they will be paid a wage of W_1. Even though this is below their marginal revenue product of labour they will continue to work for the government because there is nowhere else for them to go. ⓐ

This is clearly the reason why care workers earn low wages. They ultimately provide very valuable services to residents of care homes who would die without their help; this means they are deserving of higher wages. ⓑ

ⓔ **3/15 marks awarded.** ⓐ The diagram is only partially correct — while the curves are constructed correctly, the equilibrium wage rate is incorrect. This causes problems for the rest of the analysis as it actually shows workers at this employment level earning their marginal revenue product of labour and being paid above the competitive equilibrium wage. The written analysis, though, does demonstrate an understanding of why monopsonists are able to pay low wages. ⓑ While the student recognises the valuable work completed by those in the care sector, there is no labour market theory attached to the assertion that they should therefore be paid high wages.

Knowledge check answers

1 Individuals consider only the marginal private benefits when making decisions; they do not care about the marginal external benefits (the positive externalities) of consumption of healthcare, such as the improved productivity and economic growth that derive from a healthier workforce. As a result, equilibrium will be reached where the marginal private benefit equals the marginal private cost, at which point the marginal social benefit will exceed the marginal social cost and the social optimum will not be reached.

2 Giving money to charity does not initially appear to be rational — individuals derive no measurable utility from giving their money away and, in doing so, will be sacrificing the utility they could have enjoyed from using that money to consume a good or service. However, giving to charity can make individuals feel good about themselves. This emotional benefit does essentially bring utility to the individual; if this utility is greater than the utility that could come from purchasing a good or service, then giving to charity could be seen to be rational behaviour.

3 Small firms are likely to be profit maximisers because the managers are the owners — their salary is the profit the business makes, meaning they are incentivised by profit. It is in the large firms where managers are not necessarily the owners that managers may be incentivised to target alternative maximising objectives.

4 Public sector and voluntary organisations are likely to be utility maximisers. A public sector organisation such as the NHS is government funded and exists to maximise the utility of the general public, meaning it is motivated by cutting waiting times and providing a good quality service. Voluntary organisations such as local tennis clubs are motivated by maximising the welfare of their members.

5 Firms will exit the market as a loss is being made, causing industry supply to fall and the price to increase. The demand for each individual firm's output will increase as there are now fewer firms in the market. Firms will continue to leave the market until the price has increased to a level where average revenue equals average cost and normal profits are being earned.

6 X-inefficiency will not occur in perfect competition because firms are making only normal profits when operating at the minimum efficient scale. Competitive pressures mean organisational slack is not able to develop — any firm not operating at the lowest possible average cost would be outcompeted.

7 Railways are a good example of natural monopolies as the set-up costs of building a new network of railway lines is huge — it would be inefficient to have multiple sets of railway lines running parallel to each other.

8 Price discrimination would be difficult in the fast food industry as it is tricky to identify different groups of consumers that are willing to pay different amounts for fast food (it is often young people who may be willing to pay most, but this depends on preferences). The competitive nature of this industry also means most firms are price takers.

9 Generally, monopolistic competition would be considered better for consumers because of the greater degree of choice the market structure delivers. However, the supernormal profits made by monopolists could be used to invest in research and development and deliver more innovation (and therefore better-quality products) than in the model of monopolistic competition.

10 Monopolists are likely to benefit from economies of scale, which represent a barrier to entry. In reality, some sunk costs are likely to be incurred in order to get to a point where economies of scale can be enjoyed, making it rare for a situation where there are no barriers to entry and exit or sunk costs to occur in real-world markets.

11 Forward vertical integration, as the DIY store is at a later stage of the production process in the same industry as the lightbulb manufacturer.

12 No — in a natural monopoly it is more efficient to have only one firm operating in the industry, meaning the regulator will not be concerned by the large market share held by one firm.

13 This would increase the MPP_L, as each worker could now produce more output than before. This would increase the MRP_L, increasing the demand for labour, as each worker could now generate more revenue for a firm as a result of being able to produce a higher volume of output.

14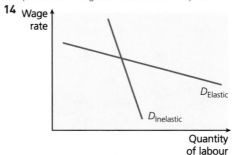

15 Individuals are likely to be more willing to supply their labour to a firm that is performing well at a lower wage rate because they believe their job is more secure, there are likely to be greater opportunities for promotion and there is a sense of status attached to working for a highly regarded firm.

16

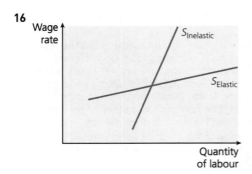

17 Changes in consumer demand — as real incomes have grown, the demand for services has increased at a faster rate than the demand for manufactured goods. Changes in comparative advantage are also important — manufacturing production now predominantly takes place in low-labour-cost countries such as China.

18 There is a high rate of owner-occupied housing in the UK — given the high costs involved in buying and selling houses, this reduces the geographical mobility of labour.

19 It is more difficult for authorities to identify informal activity in the service sector — for example, it is much harder to prove an individual is providing their services as a hairdresser visiting people's homes than it is to prove a lightbulb manufacturer is illegally producing lightbulbs.

20 It could improve the workings of the competitive labour market — supply of labour would increase in the high-wage region (London) as workers would relocate in order to enjoy higher incomes. This would cause wages in the high-wage region to fall. The demand for labour would increase in the low-wage region (Bradford) as firms would relocate to low-wage areas to take advantage of lower production costs. This would cause the wage rate in the low-wage region to increase. This should result in factor–price equalisation, but crucially depends upon the geographical mobility of workers and firms.

21 Traditionally, unionisation has been higher in the manufacturing sector than the service sector. This is partly because protecting workers' safety and conditions is needed more in manufacturing given the nature of the work conducted. As manufacturing sector employment has fallen and the service sector has boomed, this has naturally led to a decline in union membership.

22 Individuals are not aware of the full benefits of contributing to a pension because they discount future benefits when making decisions. Because they are too heavily influenced by their short-term well-being they may make the choice not to contribute to private pensions in order to enjoy a higher standard of living now, which they may regret in the future when they have a poor standard of living in retirement. Private pensions will therefore be under-consumed in a free market.

23 It would be too costly to reduce the level of pollution to zero — in the social optimum pollution will be reduced only to the point where the cost of cleaning up production is equal to the benefit derived from the associated reduction in pollution.

24 $ABCP_1$.

25 Direct costs — cost of tunnelling equipment and construction workers. Indirect costs — pollution harming residents who live nearby. Direct benefits — individuals spend less time commuting and so have more leisure time. Indirect benefits — productivity increases leading to greater tax revenue.

Index